Ink of Light

Ink of Light

by Katharine Branning

FONS VITAE

First published in 2018 by
Fons Vitae
49 Mockingbird Valley Drive
Louisville, KY 40207
http://www.fonsvitae.com
Email: fonsvitaeky@aol.com

Library of Congress Control Number: 2018932026
ISBN 978-1941610-091

The decorative calligraphy of the chapter headings reads the cherished formula *"Ya Hazret-i Mevlana"* ("Praise be to the presence of our Master"). The white calligraphy on the cover spells out the Arabic word "Nur" (Light).

Dervish drawings and cover art by Irene Kim-Ahiska.

Printed in Canada

Contents

Preface 9

Foreword 11

Chapter 1   The *Sema*: the Ceremonial Entry 15

Chapter 2   The *Sema*: the Recitation of the *Nat-i Sherif* 21

Chapter 3   The *Sema*: The *Ney* Improvisation 29

Chapter 4   The *Sema*: The *Peshrev* Musical Interlude 39

Chapter 5   The *Sema*: The Sultan Valad Procession 49

Chapter 6   The *Sema*: The Preparation to Turn
             and the 1st *Selam*: the *Sharia* 61

Chapter 7   The *Sema*: The 2nd *Selam*: the *Tariqa* 73

Chapter 8   The *Sema*: The 3rd *Selam*: the *Marifa* 85

Chapter 9   The *Sema*: The 4th *Selam*: the *Haqiqa* 97

Chapter 10 The *Sema*: The End of Turning
             and the Qur'an Reading 111

Chapter 11 The *Sema*: The *Niyaz* Dedication
             and Farewell Prayers 125

Chapter 12 The *Sema*: Departure of the *Postnishin*
             and Closure 135

Author's Note 147

Timeline of Eva de Vitray and Mevlana 152

Glossary of Terms 157

Bibliography of Works by Eva de Vitray-Meyerovitch 171

A Paris –

*Victorieuse ville lumière
des valeurs pérennes de l'humanité*

If all the trees on earth were pens,
and if the ocean with seven oceans
behind it were ink, the words of God
could not be written out to their end –

Qur'an 31:27

Preface

You hold in your hands a biographical novel of the French scholar Eva de Vitray-Meyerovitch, translator of the 13th century Sufi poet Rumi, also known as Mevlana, "Our Master."

Eva de Vitray-Meyerovitch, Paris, France, in the 1960s and 70s: a modern European woman pursuing a brilliant professional career and family life.

Jelaleddin Rumi, Konya, Turkey, in the 1250s: a teacher following his charismatic scholar father, studying and learning all he could in the cosmopolitan court of the Seljuk Empire.

Everything would appear to separate them on the surface: One was French, the other a Persian transplanted to Turkey; one was born a Christian woman in the modern era, the other a Muslim man in the Middle Ages. Yet, much united them at the same time: both were teachers and seekers of truth who communicated in the universal language of compassion and love. Each experienced a chance encounter which changed their lives and united them thereafter in spiritual and intellectual complicity.

Their dialogue across languages and cultures is related here in a series of imaginary conversations that Eva de Vitray-Meyerovitch holds with Mevlana, recalling her life story and his influence upon it. The phases of her life – childhood, university studies, marriage, war years, discovery of Islam, teaching career, travels, public advocacy, mentorship, and translation projects – all surprisingly mirror the trajectory of Mevlana's own life 700 years earlier. Both believed in the existence of a world without hate, violence, borders, or revenge; a world of peace and equality where all could meet in a field of diversity and respect.

Each conversation is preceded by a description of one of the twelve successive parts of the *sema*, the world-famous whirling ceremony of the dervishes of the Mevlevi Sufi order founded by Mevlana. These segments not only provide insight on the details of this moving ritual of moving meditation, but also set the rhythm for the mutual itinerary of Mevlana and Eva de Vitray-Meyerovitch.

So come; let us follow the lead of the humble dervish ready to begin the *sema* dance of this whirling prayer of life known as *Sufism*.

Foreword

This text presents a felicitous and rare harmony between historical fact and literary fiction. Indeed, Katharine Branning surrenders the voice of the narrator to Eva de Vitray-Meyerovitch, who addresses Rumi in a direct and intimate fashion, yet the author faithfully respects the separate historical contexts of the two heroes of this book: Rumi in the Middle East of the 13th century and Eva in Paris in the 20th. The analogies between the life stories of Eva and Rumi – on the surface quite different – are in truth quite startling; such as the parallel between the German armies during the Occupation in 1940 and the Mongol hoards which drove the family of Rumi towards Konya. The spiritual content is crucial in this book, reinforced by the fact that each chapter is introduced by a systematic presentation of the phases of the Mevlevi ritual of the "whirling dervishes."

We are not in the presence here of an umpteenth *New Age* depiction of Rumi and his works – the best-selling poet in the United States and perhaps the world – but rather of a journey towards spiritual awakening, undertaken by human beings as an essential quest for survival. It bears noting that this process took place within the framework of the Islamic tradition, whose universalism appears here in all its authenticity. *"Everything that rises must converge,"* affirms Teilhard de Chardin, and it was Sufism that united the souls of Rumi, Muhammad Iqbal (d. 1938, in whose works Eva discovered the author of the Mathnawi), and Eva. *"The Sufi is a child born in the present moment"* states a proverb, and from this point forth, the quantifiable notion of time no longer exists. Consequently, we can perceive *here and now* as the simultaneous living presence of these two exceptional human beings.

Permit me, if you may, to briefly evoke my relationship with Eva, and all that she conveyed to me. I first met her in 1984, several months before I adopted the Islamic faith, and then again in 1985 when I was seeking to join a Sufi brotherhood (*tarîqa*). Like so many others, I visited her in her Paris apartment, and we also met at several places in southern France. I recall that, imposing despite her diminutive stature, she fixed her eyes upon me with a look both serious and bemused: me, this young Western lad in search of spirituality, just as she had once been herself. She went straight to the heart of the matter. She immediately shared her experiences with reincarnation, opening herself up to something quite personal, and I realized at that moment that we shared the same life journey – although on a more modest scale, as far as I am concerned – a quest that led us to explore different spiritual traditions; a pursuit which did not leave us in peace until we had found a harbor. Even before I entered the Islamic faith, she reminded me that the Qur'an ends with this essential word: "humans" (al-nâs). Although we were both formed by Western cultural traditions, we chose not to abandon their positive elements, and were able to touch the universalism of the Islamic faith.

Lastly, I would also like to relate this anecdote which highlights the role of "mirror" which Eva fulfilled for many of Eastern cultures. A Turkish friend, a judge in Ankara who reads French, indicated to me that he discovered the work of Rumi through the books of Eva.

Eric Geoffroy
Strasbourg, December 29, 2017

Ink of Light

Chapter 1
The *Sema*: the Ceremonial Entry

The dervish is ready to begin

The dervish has spent months in training to reach this day when he will be able at last to perform the whirling turning ceremony known as the *sema*. He has memorized the symbolic meaning of every moment and every element of this spiritual oratorio. The Master Mevlana said that *"Many roads lead to God and I have chosen the way of dance and music."* He believed that whirling is a prayer done for the remembrance of God. And so the dervish whirls for Him in this concert of prayer, composed in twelve parts. The Prophet Jacob had twelve sons who founded the nation of the twelve tribes of Israel and the Prophet Jesus twelve apostles who founded the Church of Christianity. All the peoples of the Book are all united in this Cosmos, here, in the circle of the *sema*.

An atmosphere of reverent silence and tranquility prevails in the *semahane*, the hall of Celestial Sounds, where the ceremony is to be performed. The floor is round like the universe. All is in order, just as God's unity is in place in the world. At the edge of the floor is a circle of white sheepskins where the dervishes, called the *semazen*, sit. On the right is the *mutribhane*, the raised section, reserved for the musicians and singers.

Earlier, the dervish performed his ritual ablutions and then dressed in the ceremonial costume: a tall, camel-hair hat called the *sikke*, which symbolizes the tombstone of the ego, and a white robe called the *tennure*, which symbolizes the shroud of the ego. Over the *tennure* he wears a short white jacket, the *destegül*, the "bouquet of roses," held in place by a long girdle of cloth known as the *elif-named*. Covering all is a black cloak with wide, open sleeves, called the *khirka*, symbolizing his grave. On his feet are ankle-high slippers fashioned from soft leather.

The musicians enter one by one with their instruments: the *ney* flute, the *kudum* drum, the zither-like *kanun*, the *tanbur* lute, the six-stringed *ud*, the *tef* hand drum, the *kemançe* violin and the small bowed *rebab*. The chanters follow. A dervish lights a lamp and lays down a red sheepskin, known as the *post*, in front of the *mihrab* prayer niche. This red pelt represents the manifestation of God to man.

At the door to the *semahane*, the dervish locks his feet, right foot over left, and bows his head in salutation. He will whirl with other dervishes, some young like him; others old men, but always in multiples of 9, like the planets of the Milky Way. Led by the *sema-zenbashi* movement master, the dervish enters the hall alongside his fellow dervishes, who all make the same symbolic gestures. He holds his arms folded across his chest with the left hand on the right shoulder. This posture of humility is called the *niyaz*. The dervish slowly proceeds to his place at the side of the hall, assigned by rank, with the highest-ranking dervish closest to the Sheikh. The dervish kneels down on the floor atop his white sheepskin. The movement master, wearing a white *sikke*, approaches the post where the Sheikh, or *Postnishin*, will stand. The Sheikh, representing the venerable Mevlana, is the last to enter, bowing in the direction of the red sheepskin, then to the musicians and then to the dervishes. Between the red post and the musicians' section is an imaginary line on which only the Sheikh, who knows the path to divine Reality, can tread. This equator line divides the *semahane* in half, just as existence is divided into two parts: the right side is the descending sector of the material realm, and the left side is the ascending sector of the spiritual realm. The Sheikh walks along this line to the red sheepskin post and kneels down behind it, facing the dervishes. The Sheikh then opens his hands, holding his fingers straight, his palms towards his face with the two little fingers touching one another, and recites the prayer of the post, which includes a recitation of the Mevlevi lineage.

All is in place for the *sema* to begin.

Who would have thought that I, little Eva Lamacque of Boulogne-sur-Seine, would embark on such a surprising voyage through life?

I was born at the dawn of the 20th century, a time when everything was being invented and discovered: cars, planes, abstract painting, neon lights, vaccines, tractors, radar, aspirin, psychoanalysis, tea bags, escalators, atonal music and even me, a little French girl born at the cusp of this new era of modernity.

My home town, Boulogne-sur-Seine, was one of the wealthiest cities in France, the home of many pioneering entrepreneurs who transformed this Parisian suburb tucked in the western crook of the Seine River into the nest of the burgeoning aviation and automobile industries. The Renault factories along the Seine churned to produce the famed little black taxis that would soon fill the streets of Paris and New York. In these days in France more people lived on farms than in cities and the pace of horses still ruled the road, but those roaring Renault factories would soon change all of that.

My birth year of 1909 was not just a bustling time for Boulogne-sur-Seine, however. Momentous changes were happening all around the world. The Turkish parliament deposed the Ottoman Sultan Abd al-Hamid II and replaced him with his brother, Muhammad V. A new emperor in China and a new Shah in Persia took the throne. And in an unthinkable feat, the French aviator Blériot crossed the English Channel in an airplane. Imagine such a thing! The world was full of promise in that year of 1909, and yet few could guess what would soon shake the entire planet and dash this entire glorious prospect of progress into muddy trenches of despair.

My earliest memory is that of the soft cheeks of my grandmother, and it is one I can never forget. Oh, if only all aspects of life could be as soft as my grandmother's rosy cheeks! It was she who was always with me, not my mother. She hugged me in her arms and spoke to me in the purring burr of her native Scotland in a secret language that we shared together, a language of English words and soft caresses. She taught me her native language and her Protestant faith; she explained to me the sweetness of Jesus and shared with me homemade scones with orange marmalade.

She was my first gift of kindness and love. Above all, she taught me to be honest. She told me this was the most important thing in life: to be honest to the world, to others, but above all, to yourself. I remember, too, my childhood home; so spacious, with a long hall where I could run as fast as my short, chubby legs could carry me, and rooms filled with light from the tall corner windows that opened out onto a garden and the Seine River flowing nearby.

But it is those soft cheeks I remember the most. Perhaps that is why I came to you; master of poetry Mevlana Jelaleddin Rumi, for your message was as soft as my grandmother's plump cheeks which smelled of roses, just as do your words. You were filled with light, from the corner windows of your soul, shining on a path leading beyond my garden gate.

Seven hundred years before me, in 1207, you, too, grew up near a rich city, way on the other side of the world, amidst the rugged foothills of the Hindu Kush Mountains. Balkh, in what is now Afghanistan, was an ancient city of Buddhism and Zoroastrianism; rich in trade routes leading to India and China, and full of poets, graceful buildings, universities, and rose gardens. Perhaps it was worlds away from Paris and Europe, but who can say which one of us was the most fortunately born into cultural wealth? Seven hundred years ago in Balkh you were not yet a famous mystic and poet called Mevlana, *"the Master,"* nor were you yet to be called *Rumi*, the surname you took later from the term the Roman Byzantines used for Anatolia, today's Turkey, the land where you spent most of your life. No, back then, you were just a little boy named Muhammad.

Legend has it that you, too, had a grandmother, a royal princess of Khurasan, who was incomparable and loving. There, with your family in faraway Balkh, you recognized the spiritual beauty, kindness, and wisdom of women. It was your grandmother who first lit the spark of inquiry in your scholar father, Bahaeddin Valad, who in turn lit it in you. Under her care, your orphaned father grew to become a bright spiritual scholar, known to all as the "Sultan of the Learned." We certainly owe much to our grandmothers, don't we, Mevlana Jelaleddin Rumi? Perhaps they are the holiest of women, for they know the love of the past and the future at the same time.

Today, my name is both Eva and Hawwa. I carry two names, two faiths, two professions, two languages born unto me, two languages learned, and two soul mate countries. Yet for this moment, I am still little Eva Lamacque of Boulogne-sur-Seine near Paris, France, hugged by the loving arms of her grandmother and ready to discover the promise of the world around me.

Chapter 2
The *Sema*: the Recitation of
the *Nat-i Sherif*

The dervish is ready to listen

The *sema* ceremony begins. When everyone is seated, a *Hafiz*, a scholar who has memorized the entire Qur'an by heart, recites a eulogy to the Prophet, known as the *Nat-i Sherif*, which is preceded by the words *"Ya Hazret-i Mevlana, haqq dost"*: "Praise be to the presence of our Master, the friend of Truth." This prayer of noble praise was written by Mevlana and was set to music composed by the celebrated musician Buhuriz Mustafa Itri Efendi in the late 17th century. The dervishes solemnly listen to its moving notes, which are sung *a capella* and without rhythm by a solo standing chanter. The *Nat-i Sherif* praises not only Muhammad, but all the Prophets who exemplify love by their messages and lives, as well as Mevlana. To praise them is to praise God, who created them all.

After the Nat, the small *kudum* kettle drums are struck a few times. The sound symbolizes Allah's command "BE!" as related in the Holy Qur'an, Chapter 36, verse 82: *"Verily, when He intends a thing, His command is be and it is!"*

My white lace collar was pressed, my book bag packed, my light brown hair tied back with a blue ribbon, my black shoes polished and my slate wiped clean, ready to learn my letters, on this, my very first day of school.

I came from a well-to-do family: education, wealth, and prestige were all mine for the taking. In my pampered world, I thought everyone lived like I did. I ate *madeleines* with my tea and rode on a wooden rocking horse with a silver silk mane and tail. And, as were all little girls of upper class families, I was sent to a private Catholic school, where discipline was strict and educational standards were the highest, and where all the little girls were just like me.

As an innocent five-year-old wandering down the path to school on that clear, sunny September morning in 1914, I was totally unaware that one month earlier the world had entered into a deadly cataclysm that would pave the way for major political changes and revolutions in many countries. Empires would collapse and 16 million souls would perish over the next four years, and yet all I was concerned about on that bright morning was whether my pencils were sharp enough and if I would be lonely without my grandmother at my side.

As much as I wanted to wander into the world beyond my garden gate to discover this new world called *learning*, I still approached the hulking school building with trepidation. I soon discovered, however, that I loved school and learning, and that I was very, very good at my lessons, and always got to sit at the head of the class in the front row of seats.

I enjoyed participating fully in the life of a young Catholic girl. I loved the Virgin Mary and Jesus with all my heart, and prayed to them each day. Faith became a strong and mysterious force in my life. I proudly celebrated my first communion and eagerly looked forward to participating in the Month of Mary festivities each year with my grandmother. During this special month of May, you meditated on the qualities of Mary and tried to take inspiration from her by practicing each day a different virtue of hers. From a very young age, I was curious about the spiritual world, a world I imagined filled with fluttering angels, where Jesus reigned and where God was a sort of Mother Superior. I even thought, as many young girls do, that I wanted to become a Carmelite nun myself, to be just like the *bonnes soeurs* nuns who taught me at school, dressed in their black robes and their tall, starched white hats.

I was sent to the very best schools. My first school was not far from my home in Boulogne-sur-Seine, but afterwards I attended a school in the shadows of the gargoyles of the majestic Cathedral of Notre Dame in the center of Paris. This academy was filled with *mademoiselles* from the finest families of France, all here to be taught to become models of virtue that could find the best husbands possible. Days were filled with a repetitive routine of *matins* and lessons, but I clearly remember one day different than all the others. It was the day I heard the colossal, 13-ton Emmanuel Bell of Notre Dame pealing so madly that I was certain it could be heard resounding in every corner of France. It was Monday, November 11, 1918. We were all let go from school to join the jubilant crowds streaming down the boulevards, where all Paris was jumping in air and singing and shouting that the war was over at last, this war of horrors raged in the hell fields of Verdun of which a little nine-year-old girl in a convent school could never have begun to imagine.

Discipline was exceedingly rigid at school, and behavior counted for 1/5th of your weekly grade. We wore uniforms and the *bonnes soeurs* would rap our knuckles with a wide ruler if we did not sit up straight or heed their warnings. My timid German teacher was different; he was so kind and I always admired his dignity and love of literature. I may have been a well-mannered girl and devout, but I did have a streak of the devil in me. I would run to the pastry shop after mass to buy myself an *éclair* for a treat – a minor transgression, mind you, but still worthy of a knuckle rap. But above all, I asked questions, way too many questions for my own good.

I had always been a fiercely independent child, and never could be told what to do, much less what to think. Even at a young age I had already developed a mind of my own, a French mind that enquires and debates; a mind of a child of the descendants of the Enlightenment. At school I had the prickly habit of always asking the questions that one apparently should not have been thinking, much less asking. When I was around 12, I went to confession and spoke to the priest about something that had been preoccupying me for a while. *"Father, I often dream that I have been experiencing situations that are somehow already familiar to me, as if I had already lived them in the past. There is just something inside of me that tells me that I am here today with something more inside of me than what I am today. Do you believe that it is possible to think that we have lived past lives before we came here?"* His answered my innocent question with an angry dismissal, and I went away from the confessional booth frustrated, and, frankly, a bit angry that my question had not been honored for its value.

I was born a Catholic, just as I was born with brown hair. I did not choose to be baptized, to celebrate my first communion, to learn the catechism. It was the fate of my birth. Yet, I was always curious about the world around me when I was a little girl: why sparks danced in the fire, why a vacuum bottle could be both hot and cold, why waves moved up and down, why spiders had eight legs and bugs six, why both the sky and the sea were blue. I was always curious about those other lives, those before me perhaps, but certainly those of the world around me. Early on, I realized that life is about wanting to know more. Questioning. What is this about? What is this not about? Why do we like this? Do we like this? So it was not surprising that I began to wonder what was behind all those words I was made to memorize in catechism class, about a God and the man Jesus I would never know. I could feel God, yes, just like I could feel my grandmother's kiss and the fur of my pet kitten, but I wanted more. I wanted to see Him; I wanted to talk with Him. But with my words, not those of the priests.

With the arrival of my teenage years, this questioning became more pronounced. I found it increasingly difficult to accept the authoritarian boundaries that were imposed upon me at school. As many teens, I became increasingly contrary. My rebellion manifested itself with a growing discontentment with those pat answers, daring me to venture outside the lines of religious dogma. I began creating many problems for my teachers with what they perceived was impertinence, but what I considered pure intellectual inquiry. I began to suffer from the conformity of thought and actions of everyone that surrounded me in school, and when I would go to the priests to speak to them about my problems, they would always simply respond that it was not good for me to think such things and that I needed to pray to God to have these doubts removed from my mind. This was not the type of answer I wanted to hear; in fact, they were not answers at all, but vague mumblings and this angered me. No one was going to tell me that I did not merit to be given an answer to valid questions.

The authoritarian attitude of the priests and *bonnes soeurs* created all the more problems in that it was in conflict with the most important life lesson taught to me by my beloved grandmother, which was to be above all honest with one's self and the world. I could not just dismiss all these things that were bothering me, for that would have been morally or intellectually dishonest. I could no longer look at the *bonnes soeurs* or the priests in the same way as before when I was a young girl celebrating the Month of Mary.

Did you ever question the things taught to you, Mevlana? I somehow think that you did not; I sense that you were a very well-behaved little boy named Muhammad and a most respectful student. The time for questioning came much later for you than it did for me.

While I was learning about the lives and deeds of the Catholic saints from the *bonnes soeurs,* you were learning of the Muslim saints while sitting on the knee of your father. When I was reading Molière and Hugo, you were reading about the Prophet Muhammad. Your teacher was your own father, the religious scholar and jurist Bahaeddin Valad, and you learned at his feet all the concepts of Islam. From an early age, he began calling you "Jelaleddin," meaning "Majesty of the Faith." Then came the day when the approach of the brutal Mongol warriors, intent on conquering the world, disrupted the security of your existence. When you were five years old, instead of heading off to school like I did, your family was forced to take flight westwards from Balkh to escape the razing path of these encroaching hoards of destruction. While I was safe and pampered in my bourgeois apartment near Paris, you were on dusty roads fleeing for your lives. While I was savoring sugared cakes and hot chocolate from the fancy pastry shops of Paris, you were gnawing on dried figs and unleavened flatbread, with only curdled milk and bulgur soup to fill your starving stomach as you escaped along rocky, unknown roads. You had a childhood of upheaval, not one of coddled lessons in a convent school in the shadow of the finest cathedral in the land.

Your hometown was reduced to ruins by the Mongols two years after you left, burned to the ground with thousands of people killed, just like innocents who were being killed in the trenches of Verdun during my youth. During those years, you traveled throughout Muslim lands, encountering majestic mountains and beautiful plains. Along the way, you visited major cities and met well-known Sufis and scholars of the time. You first went to Samarkand, then to Nishapur, then to Baghdad, Mecca, Medina, Damascus, Malatya, and Erzincan; always in motion to outrun those Mongols and to try to find a safe haven. At last you found a home in Anatolia, the land now known as Turkey. You arrived there around the age of 15 and settled with your family in the city of Karaman for seven years, where a local ruler, Musa, opened a school for your father Bahaeddin.

Yes, Mevlana, you were born in an epoch of troubled times, just as I was: a century of grandiose duels. The Crusaders from the west invaded the Middle East and the waves of the giant ocean of Genghis Khan and the Mongols invaded from the east, both destroying all in their path. When we were children, your world was being ripped apart by the Mongols and my Europe, the supposed Holy Empire of civilization, was shattering into chaos, where brothers tore at each other from disease-ridden, muck-filled trenches while their lungs were being seared with mustard gas. We grew up in worlds filled with strife, you and I; is it any wonder we desperately turned to a quest for love for the rest of our lives?

I turned to love, yes, but first I turned to honesty, as taught to me by my grandmother. I decided to take a step back from the stricture and dogma of the Church. It was an especially happy day for me when I graduated from high school and walked out the tall door of that Catholic convent school for the last time, leaving behind all my frustrations and unanswered questions.

It was now 1926 and I was ready to go to the university. A new life would begin there; of that I was certain, one that encouraged debate and discussion, and one where answers would be found. I eagerly awaited the fall to arrive, and spent my time with my friends enjoying the pleasures of summer days in Paris. On a stroll one late afternoon through the Latin Quarter of Paris, I passed in front of a building which had just been inaugurated, not too far from the Cathedral of Notre Dame. It was a place of worship, they told me, but it certainly looked nothing like Notre Dame. It was a Muslim mosque. A stout square minaret decorated with blue mosaic tiles jutted into the sky of the 5th arrondissement, and its thick, solid walls were made of white adobe trimmed in green. This *Grande Mosquée de Paris*, the Great Mosque of Paris, had been built in honor of the 100,000 infantry Muslim skirmishers from the French colonies of Africa who had perished in World War I. As I stood outside its entry gate carved with filigree tracery and peeked into its courtyard garden lined with graceful columns and waterways radiating from a bubbling fountain at its center, I thought to myself what a curious place of worship it seemed. Little did I know that such a place would one day become my home; the haven for all my questions.

Chapter 3
The *Sema*: The *Ney* Improvisation

The dervish is ready to yearn

At the conclusion of the *Nat*, the sound of the kettle drums breaks the silence, followed by the piercing sound of a solo reed flute, the *ney*. The dervishes, now kneeling, listen to the musical improvisation of the flute, which represents divine breath and evokes the first breath which gives all creatures life. The plaintive song of the *ney* expresses its melancholy that it has been separated from the reed bed in the pond, just as the dervish is sad to be separated from God. The song evokes the famous opening lines of Mevlana's poetic masterpiece, the *Masnavi*: "*Hearken to the reed flute and how it cries, lamenting its banishment from its home...*"

In the fall of 1927, I once again took an unknown path on the adventure of learning, only this time I was not afraid: I knew that the University of Paris would open doors to me into a new dimension of knowledge that would surely be able to provide the answers to my questions that the *bonnes soeurs* and the priests were never able to give me.

As all new university students, I was like a child in a candy shop with so many enticing courses and books. Which ones should I choose? I yearned to learn everything, and, like so many students at the beginning of their university years, I was open to everything. Despite my frustration with my Catholic education and the strict dogma of the Church, I still remained interested in spiritual issues. Ever curious, I began to investigate other religious traditions in courses at the university to discover their truths, for I could no longer accept that the Catholic Church insisted that it was the only path to salvation. I studied Indian philosophy and Sanskrit at the Institute of Oriental Languages, familiarly called "*Langues O*" by the students, a marvelous institution which had been founded in the era of the French Revolution in 1795. It was there I fell in love with the *Bhagavad Gita*, which would remain a major source of inspiration for the rest of my life. I explored Buddhism, and, although I could admire its universal compassion, its love of animals and its lack of dogma, I could not connect with it intellectually. In the end, I chose to study two soundly traditional and respectable subjects for my degree: the law and Ancient Greek.

However, it was not easy for me to let go of my Catholic upbringing. I still attended mass, but I continued to question the dogma of the Church, now enriched with a critical and ever-expanding eye, thanks to my study of other religious traditions. I had studied enough history to know, for example, that the first known texts of the Evangelists dated from the 4th century and that they were translations, not the original words of Jesus. I had learned, too, from my studies of Ancient Greek that there could be a significant difference between a Greek phrase and a phrase coming from a Semitic language. The question of the veracity of translations and the challenge of Babel began to intrigue me. I suppose the translation point in the New Testament that bothered me the most was the rendering of the Aramaic words of Jesus, *"I am the son of Man and the servant of God"* into Greek as *"I am the son of God."* This was not the same thing at all, and, from this, the prophetic voice of the man Jesus had become transformed into the Christ the Lord of the Catholic Church, which was again, not the same thing at all. All began to seem like manipulation and it became increasingly difficult for me to accept it. I wished that my grandmother were there to speak to me about the Protestant faith in which she was raised, so much more direct and pure than the Catholic one, but she was no longer here. I wanted to be honest with myself, as my grandmother taught me, but I began to doubt that my questions about belief would ever be answered. It was becoming challenging for me to remain a Catholic and to just shut my eyes to all these nagging questions; to neatly put them into parentheses when I took communion or recited prayers. I was expected to be a brilliant student, honest in my writings and research and exams, but at the same time, I felt as if I were cheating each time I went to mass.

I may have been questioning, but I was also studying the texts of law with diligence. There were few girls in my class, as the law was a male-dominated field at this time. I finished my law degree at the age of 21, and, with a certain pride, I can tell you that I graduated first in my class, ahead of all those male students!

In all the ebullience of my early university years and all this searching, I did find one thing that was true and indisputable: love. It is a miracle, I believe, when two people can look themselves in the eyes and know that they are looking at the other half of their destiny. Such was the case when I first looked into the face of Lazare Meyerovitch. Everything united us and everything separated us. We shared the same year of birth and an identical curiosity about the world around us. I studied law and philosophy and he studied engineering. I was a Catholic daughter of France from an old family; he was a Jew from Riga in Latvia who had immigrated to France to study at the University. I spoke French with the clipped bourgeois accent of upper-class Paris and English with the burr of northern Scotland; he spoke Latvian and Russian and his French had a heavy Slavic accent. Yet love united us. Oh, I know I am not particularly pretty: I am short and plain and have a high squeaky voice; but he saw another beauty in me. He was different and exciting in my eyes – and so exceptionally bright – but above all, he was considerate and courteous. I knew I would never be bored

31

with this man and we married at the age of 22; so young, perhaps, and yet we were so eager to share everything. Love seemed more meaningful than any truth we could possibly learn at the University. I now carried an unwieldly and incredibly un-French name, but I was so happy and in love that it didn't matter that people had such trouble pronouncing it!

Although not purposely intended, the day of our marriage was perhaps the first time I first truly challenged my faith traditions. My husband was an agnostic – how odd that I should marry someone who was not concerned about searching for God like I was – but in his own way, he, too, had rejected the traditions of the family faith. He never forced me to convert to Judaism so that our children would be raised Jewish, for as an agnostic, this was really not an issue for him. Although I was a believer in the importance of a spiritual life, I never felt that his lack of belief would in any way be a problem for our marriage, and it was not. He was a calm and gentle man, and completely supportive of my convictions and questions. I knew we would be happy together; of that I was certain. My beloved Scottish grandmother, born an Anglican, had converted to Catholicism to marry my grandfather, so I was not the first one in the family to have married outside of the faith, and I suppose the example of her marriage was one of my first lessons in the underlying spiritual connections between religions.

Around this time I began to do translations to earn money, for as a newlywed, there was so much to purchase to set up house! The English that I had learned on my beloved grandmother's knee – I spoke it before French – became a valuable commodity for me on the job market. I studied during the day and did my translations at night, and, luckily for me, hard work does not faze me. My very first published translation was an amusing memoir relating the lifestyle of the Chinese mandarins under the Manchu Dynasty. It was published in 1935, the same year my husband became a naturalized French citizen. So proudly did I sign that book as "*Eva Meyerovitch*"!

I may have finished my law degree, but I still continued to look for the answers to all those nagging questions about my faith. I now believed that I could find them in the study of Greek philosophy. However, after the reassuring rationale of my studies in law and the ancient Greek language, delving into Greek philosophy stirred up so many conflicting thoughts in my mind that all the uneasiness I felt towards the Catholic Church rose to the surface and became unbearable. Plato fascinated me above all the others. I felt that it was perhaps there in Plato's texts that I would at last find my answers to my troubled relation with God.

With Plato, it seemed as if a wide door had opened and a gust of fresh inspiration entered my brain. When I first read his *Symposium*, unfathomable questions surged forth from within me: Do we have a soul? Is the soul immortal? Here he was asking the exact very same questions that I had asked the *bonnes soeurs*. What does it mean to learn? How is it that we desire to know something for which we have no preconceived idea? And why, oh why, are we so attracted to this idea of an Absolute Being that is so beyond us?

Plato taught me to look for truth. Above all, with Plato, I was able to devote myself to the study of the theory of reminiscence, or as the Greeks called it, *anamnesis*. It is based on a simple postulate: before our birth, our souls have traveled through other worlds where they were able to contemplate ideas in all their perfection – ideas such as justice, beauty, harmony, and, at the top of this hierarchy, the idea of goodness. Our birth into this world is a shock for the soul, which basically wipes out all that our anterior lives learned before our birth. Yet in reality, man, by nature immortal, inherently carries inside him all these truths and qualities, but he is not aware of them. What one perceives as learning, then, is actually only the recovery of what one has forgotten from previous existences. Plato described that the recall of memories and the rediscovery of our understanding come back to us in the form of dreams. I vividly recalled my question to the priest at school about my dream of reincarnation, and how I had been dismissed as having foolish thoughts, and now I discovered that the most famous Greek philosopher of all was providing me a structured debate and analysis of this early intuition I had concerning the question.

I took many courses in psychology as well so that I could better understand the symbolism of Plato and also found that psychology offered me many theoretical answers to my questioning of the Catholic faith and gave me a better understanding of Plato. Plato also taught me the important lesson of forms, and the reality of what we perceive in our world. One of Plato's chief ideas is his belief that the world is made up of reflections of more perfect and ideal forms. The material world – the one we see, touch, hear, and smell – is really just comprised of half-seen images of the reality of ideal forms. Relying on physical senses alone is not enough to see reality. A form – whether it is a bird, a tree or a dog, is only a partial explanation of what it is and the true knowledge which lies behind it. To illustrate the situation of man on this earth and his idea of forms, Plato uses the parable of the cave in his main work, *The Republic*. The people who live in the cave – our world – can only see the shadows on the wall of what is represented. Man is enchanted by a wall upon which he enjoys the reflections of the sunrays until the day he discovers that what he is seeing is only a reflection on the wall of a light source coming from a different and higher place. From Plato I learned that it might be possible for me to have a higher understanding of truth if I could flee the cave of Catholicism. In the end, however, I knew that the nourishment I was seeking would still have to come from my relationship with God and that no book, not even by Plato, could contain all of the answers. At least I thought that, Mevlana, until the day I read *your* book.

Mevlana, I often wonder what your university studies must have been like, and if you were a questioner like I am. I try to imagine what books you read and what insights you received. Did you read Plato, as well? The exodus road was fraught and bumpy for you and your family: you traveled throughout the Middle East, and I never left Paris. I wonder what it would have been like to travel throughout the world like you did and see the things you did and learn along the way. After you settled in Karaman, you, too, married young, at the age of 17, to the lovely Gevher, "the Pearl," and the next spring, your first son, Alaeddin, was born. Later, a second son, Sultan Valad, came along. As is customary in the Middle Eastern culture, you now began to be called after the place where you lived: Jelaleddin Muhammad *al-Rumi*. "Rumi" was the Arabic term used to denote "Romans," meaning those from the West, and was by extension applied to Anatolia, which had only recently been wrested away from the Byzantine Romans by the Seljuk Turks. When you were 22, about the same age as I was when I received my law degree, the Seljuk Sultan Alaeddin Keykubad, aware of your father's reputation, invited him to move from Karaman to the capital city of Konya to teach in a religious academy. This visionary sultan sought to transform Konya into the cultural core of the Middle East, and, in many ways, he succeeded, erecting fine monuments and attracting prominent scholars and poets to work there.

Your family settled in Konya where you would remain for the rest of your life. Your father lectured to packed classes in the Altinapa Medrese and became even more venerated. Alas, when you were 24, just about the age when I began to read Plato, your father Bahaeddin died. This distinguished Islamic scholar had been your only teacher up to this point, but it was evident you still needed more education. You took over teaching your father's classes at the medrese, hesitantly, since you felt inadequately prepared. Soon after your father's death, his leading disciple, Seyyid Burhaneddin, "the Knower of Secrets," suddenly appeared in Konya, announcing that he had come to continue your education. He knew you held much promise, and indeed, under his guidance, you first discovered Arabic poetry and sciences and began to study different subjects. Your mind was opening, just like mine did when I first entered the University. Above all, Burhaneddin encouraged you to explore mysticism, the belief that personal communication and union with God could be achieved through intuition, introspection, and sudden insight, as opposed to the more traditional forms of orthodox worship. Although you had learned much from the mainstream theological inclinations of your father, you began to find conventional theology and classical learning unsatisfying and too preoccupied with formalism. Burhaneddin pushed you to open your mind and to question, but most importantly, he also encouraged you to go to Syria to study with the finest scholars of the day. There, you began to compose poetry in Arabic, and your range of literary skills increased exponentially. You stayed in Aleppo for four years, and when you returned to Konya at the age of 29, you were an accomplished scholar. In order to reach even higher levels of illumination, Burhaneddin then made you fast and complete three exhausting periods of 40 days each in intense seclusion and meditation like Jesus did when he retreated to the desert. When you finished this trial, Burhaneddin told you: *"Now go and decorate the souls of men with fresh life and unending mercy; revive all those lifeless bodies in this world with your love and thought."* His mission completed, Burhaneddin left Konya and retired to Kayseri in order that you could shine on your own. In many ways our two educational paths have been similar, for both of us benefitted from matchless teachers who pushed us to question everything and to develop into the finest intellectuals we could be.

In my life at this time there was even more joy than the learning adventure with Plato, the happy days of a newlywed and my first published translation. Our first son was born in the spring of 1938, and very soon after, we moved into the apartment on the rue Claude Bernard in the 5th *arrondissement* of Paris, which would remain my home for the rest of my life. Situated on the top floor, its 5th floor windows offered a picturesque view over the famed rooftops of Paris. It was in such a stimulating neighborhood, full of prestigious learning institutions such as the Sorbonne, l'Ecole Normale Supérieure and the Curie Research Foundation. The spacious grounds of the Hospital of Val-de-Grâce, built by King Louis XIV, were just behind my street and the bustling open air food market on the rue Mouffetard but a stone's throw away. Best of all, my apartment was located between two of the most magnificent parks in Paris: the Jardin de Luxembourg and the Jardin des Plantes. How I loved to take the baby in his buggy to the Luxembourg Gardens and stroll along its formal manicured lawns, tree-lined promenades and colorful flowerbeds in the shadow of the ornate fountain built by Queen Marie de Médicis! My baby son giggled with delight as he watched the model sailboats in its circular water basin and the Punch and Judy puppets in their tall green theater boxes.

With the prospect of delving more into the study of Plato, a cooing baby on my lap, the warm gaze of my husband upon me and my new home, my world glowed with love and contentment. Peace was in my heart and I felt the world was a bright promise waiting for me to discover. Little could I have imagined in those blissful days that the distant rumbling of tanks would soon bring this contentment to a cruel halt.

Chapter 4
The *Sema*: The *Peshrev* Musical Interlude

The dervish is ready to submit

After the *ney* prelude, an instrumental work called the *peshrev* begins. It is played in the 28-beat *devrikebir* rhythmic pattern. With the first beat of the *peshrev*, the Sheikh and the kneeling dervishes say aloud "Allah," bow their heads forward and strike the floor with their palms, indicating the day of the Last Judgment and the Sirat Bridge that is crossed to get from this world to Paradise. It is said that this bridge is as thin as a hair and as sharp as a razor.

The dervishes rise to their feet, signifying that everything comes into being following Allah's command, "Be!" and, at the same time, it represents the dead rising from the grave.

During the *sema*, the dervishes will strive to reach the state of flawlessness and union with the Truth, in order to be spiritually one with God: an *insan-i kamil*, a perfect being.

The carefree life of my university days was now over. With my law degree in hand and a home to build, the time had come to establish a career. I obtained a position as the administrative manager of the laboratory of the chemist Frédéric Joliot-Curie and his wife Irène, who was the daughter of the celebrated scientists Marie and Pierre Curie. This young couple was famous as well, for they, too, had jointly won the Nobel Prize for Chemistry in 1935 for their discovery of artificial radioactivity. Building on the work of Marie and Pierre Curie, they performed alchemic magic by turning one element into another by creating radioactive nitrogen from boron. What excitement it was for me to be working for Nobel Prize winners! I was very happy in their lab, for Monsieur Frédéric was so kind to me, always teasing me and so simple and natural despite his brilliant mind. I think he secretly held as much admiration for my knowledge of Shakespeare as I did for his chemical formulas. The couple was working on the development of the atomic bomb at that time. Monsieur Frédéric was trying to establish the criteria for the creation of a successful nuclear reactor using heavy water, which was a key substance for the transformation of natural uranium into plutonium. I wrote many a letter to the Ministry of War to solicit the use of a piece of land in the Sahara Desert where he could carry out his experiments, but these letters always were answered with curt refusals.

Our serene world was suddenly upturned in the lovely spring of 1940. On May 10, Hitler activated his plan to inflict a total defeat of the French Army in northern France by entering France via the Netherlands and Belgium. Seven panzer divisions of German tanks rolled unimpaired towards the Meuse River. The next day, on May 11, Frédéric called me at home on the phone and spoke quickly and firmly: *"I cannot talk now or say much. The Germans are about to enter Paris. Just take your son, your money and any jewels you may have and come to the lab at once. There will be a car here which will take us far from Paris."*

I was stunned but moved quickly. I closed up our apartment on the rue Claude Bernard. Would I ever see it again? I was alone at this time, for my husband, now that he had become a French citizen, was away completing his obligatory military service. How would I get word to him, and would he be able to join us? I could not think of that right now; I just had to concentrate on Monsieur Frédéric's words and to getting my little boy to safety. We joined in what came to be known as the "Great Exodus," in which over 4/5 of the population of Paris fled the city almost overnight. Millions of people took to the roads in any form of transport they could find. Cars, pushcarts, and bicycles were piled high with household belongings, with mattresses, kettles, and pets spilling out onto the roads leading south. The traffic jams starting at the southern Porte d'Orléans of Paris were horrendous, as you can imagine, with almost two million people fleeing Paris all at once. It was beastly hot as well, adding to all the confusion and chaos of this colossal human caravan. All feared that the Germans were going to bomb Paris, as their adroit propaganda had led everyone to believe. Most set out with little idea of where they were going, but all sought to put as much distance as possible between themselves and the advancing army.

Hitler's tanks reached the Meuse River by May 12, and, on June 14, the Parisians who had remained in the city awakened to loud-speakers bellowing out in a heavily-accented French that a curfew had been established starting that evening so that the German troops could enter and occupy Paris. How fortunate I was to not to have heard that indignity!

I was dropped off by the Joliot-Curies in the Loiret region at the home of one of my childhood friends. What I didn't know on the journey south was that sitting on the floor of the back seat of the car at my feet next to my little suitcase was the only bottle of heavy water in existence at the time, swifted away by Monsieur Frédéric from his lab. Had we been stopped, he would have certainly committed suicide before letting on what was in that bottle, so dedicated was he to his research. All the heritage of my name-sake Eva Curie, one of the most brilliant women ever to have lived, was in that bottle of heavy water at my feet. After dropping me off, the Joliot-Curies continued on, and later I learned that Monsieur Frédéric had successfully managed to smuggle all his research documents to England before the Germans raided his lab.

What was I to do now and how was I to survive? I had to submit to the hard reality of survival in a time of war. I was 30 years old, and there was no question of returning to Paris as the Germans were there, and, with the Joliot-Curies gone, I no longer had a job.

I decided to settle with my little son, barely two years old, in the town of Brive in the Corrèze region of southwestern France, which was located in the Free Zone. I received news there that my husband had crossed into Spain to join the Forces Françaises Libres, which were composed of volunteers coming from all corners of France and the colonies to fight to liberate France from the Nazi yoke. The Free French Forces refused to accept the armistice with the Nazis signed by the Pétain government of Vichy. I received no further news of him for the entire four years of the war. Every day was lived in anxiety, for I never knew if my husband was dead or alive.

The Corrèze region was full of *maquisards*, the rural guerilla bands of French Resistance fighters who took to the mountains and came out of the brush at night to lead their raids. In fact, the Limousin region, which comprised the Corrèze where I was living, was probably the largest and most active group of all the *maquis* of France. I helped them in whatever way I could, as I felt it was my duty and it also made me feel closer to my husband, as I would like to think that there was a woman somewhere out there who would show him kindness and save his life if he were in need. I hid rebel *maquisards* in my little house and fed them whatever I could, which wasn't much. I lived in total fear of being discovered, especially after the Germans took control of Brive at the end of 1942, for my house was located next to the German commander's headquarters. Countless times I would be awakened in the middle of the night by the cries of people being tortured for information. One night, this could be me, I thought; but I carried on helping the *maquisards* for the love of my husband and for France and to end this war as soon as possible.

One still night at the beginning of the war, I almost did meet death. With no notice, one night the Gestapo police came banging at 3am on the door of my little house. They were looking for my husband who had apparently come to Brive right after the Armistice was signed in late June 1940, before leaving for Spain and then on to London to join General de Gaulle. Not only was my husband in the Resistance, but he was also a Jew, so that made his capture particularly coveted. I opened the door to find two loutish officers standing there, who brusquely pushed me aside and barged in, searched the rooms and asked me where I was hiding my husband. In a split second I knew that in order to save my life I had

42

to think fast and smart and show no fear, although my heart was racing so fast that I was certain they could have heard it pounding across the room. I knew that if they took me and tortured me to get information, I would surely give up what I knew about my fellow Resistance fighters and their denunciation would mean certain death for them. No one resists torture – if those cries from the nearby Gestapo station were any indication – and these two officers looked like monsters capable of anything. I reasoned that if they took me as a prisoner and deported me, my little boy would die and my husband would be left with no one to come home to if he survived after all these years of trial. Somewhere, from deep inside of me, I pulled up a miracle. In German – a language I knew only from my studies with the *bonnes soeurs* and my philosophy texts at the university – I pieced together enough words to bark out a response. From what buried corner of my brain did that ever come, I still ask myself after all these years, other than a corner jostled by a divine intervention by an angel? I growled out, trying to sound as coarse as possible, for it seemed this would be the only register they would comprehend. I glared at them and snarled: *"That husband of mine? Humph! That shithead left me here alone for some other broad and I don't give a damn what happens to his lousy ass!"*

I certainly never spoke such vulgar language in my life; much less in German – if the *bonnes soeurs* could have heard me! – but I knew that this would be the only way I could get through to those two brutes. They looked at each other, and one poked his buddy in the ribs with his elbow and let out a guffaw. *"This one certainly has nothing to hide!"* and laughing, they both left, slamming the door behind them. I stood there transfixed, unable to believe that in less than one second, I had faced death and then saved not only my life but the life of my son, my husband and countless others. I stood there panting, shaking with such force that when I calmed down I saw that my fist in my pocket had crushed to bits one of the most precious objects I owned: a package of cigarettes that I used to barter for bread. Still to this day I cannot truly understand what happened there in the deep cortex of my brain – but it was a miracle, of that I am certain.

The war went on and on. The world I lived in was so dark; black dark, and I despaired. I knew, however, that to keep my sanity I had to hold onto the belief that I could come out of this turmoil intact, and that occidental Europe would rise from this mayhem and find the Enlightenment of Voltaire once again. I had to believe that in all this darkness we would find a way to a world where there is no hurt. I had to hold on to the fact that God's love can reveal itself in affliction perhaps more clearly than in happy days. I had to hold on to the conviction that grace and reason can rule instead of guns and stomping boots, yet this world of peace seemed so far, far, away, especially on the day I heard the thunderous stomping of boots in front of my home, which still echoes in my ears today.

Yes, one day I heard the determined cadence of marching boots and saw a large battalion of German soldiers passing down the road in front of my house. Shortly after I learned that this brigade was responsible for committing what was probably the most heinous crime of the entire war: the Massacre of Oradour-sur-Glane.

Following the D-Day invasion of June 6, 1944 – a day inscribed forever in history, the day when the resolute bravery of those intrepid Americans achieved an inconceivable exploit for humanity – all the German troops in the south of France were ordered to move north to try to stop the Allied advance. Such was the brigade I saw passing by my door, which first stopped in the nearby village of Tulle. Perhaps sensing that the end was near, the panicked soldiers, in a last desperate act, rounded up all the men of the village, hanged 100 of them in the main square and then sent off another 150 to perish in the Dachau concentration camp. Their rampage continued the next day. They marched on to the village of Oradour, where they locked 247 women and 205 children into the village church. They led the men of the village to barns and sheds where they were machine-gunned down *en masse* with no mercy. The village church was then set on fire, and the women and children who tried to escape the flames were shot dead on the spot. In a few hours more than 600 innocent men, women, and children were massacred in a carnage that seemed to have been prompted in retaliation for a German officer who had been taken prisoner by the Resistance fighters and who was supposedly being held in this village. To this day, the smell of the embers of that burned church and the image of its innocent dead has never left my mind or heart.

And you, Mevlana, you must have seen much of the same horror during your young years, when the Mongols burned, sacked, and destroyed entire cities in their path, simply for the joy of killing and destruction. How did you react to such horror, and how did you find the courage to continue on? The army of Genghis Khan swept down upon Central Asia, burning every city to the ground and torturing practically every human being they came across in their mad fury to raze all vestige of civilization. What brings man to such hatred, such mania for power?

Yet in this world of hunger and fear, I carried on. I survived, but I was constantly hungry and tired. There was so little to eat, and what I had, I gave to my young boy first, for he needed to grow up strong. I found a job as an archivist at the Phillips factory, but I still did not have enough money to live on. To make ends meet, I put an ad in the local paper offering tutoring services in Latin, Greek, English, or French. I did not suspect, however, that the one person who would answer my ad would be a German officer wanting to improve his French. I did not want to accept his offer on moral grounds, but he made me understand that I had no choice. And my little boy, suffering from malnutrition, needed milk, and for that, I would have sacrificed anything. I swallowed my dignity and accepted to tutor him. Luckily I could save face in front of the people with whom I lodged by going to his hotel to give the lessons, but I was petrified to be alone with him in his room. However, all went well; he was courteous and kind, and spoke with sadness of his brother who had been killed on the Russian front.

At last, in August, thanks to the bravery of those thousands of gutsy Americans on a June day like none other, France was liberated. On that joyful day, I stepped out of my house and saw French soldiers rounding up Germans, and among the soldiers they were loading onto a truck as prisoners of war was my officer student. I immediately stepped forward and spoke up for him to the Allied officers, telling them that I could attest to his integrity and that his life should be spared. I don't know why I did that; after the recent horror of Oradour I should have felt the need for vindication, but all I felt was the need for mercy. I thought of my kind German professor when I was at school with the *bonnes soeurs;* I thought of the inspiring texts of Hegel and Kant and Nietzsche I read at the university and it just seemed that after this war where I had seen so much hatred and horror, perhaps one simple act of kindness and love could be my small part in reconstructing a peace between our two countries. If there is one thing I had learned after all these long years of hardship is that one must never be afraid to show love before hate. *Love is never wrong.* I was holding the hand of my young son while I pleaded with the officers, and when I looked down at it, I thought of all the little hands of the lost children of Oradour. I felt that this tiny gesture of forgiveness – the supreme lesson taught to us by Jesus – was owed to those tiny innocent martyrs so that their lives would not have been sacrificed in hatred. Living a life guided by mercy seemed to me to be the only salvation to heal from this war, and so I squeezed the little hand of my son tightly, closed my eyes and forgave that German officer and all the others in this terrible cataclysm of horror that was World War II.

A few days later, due to my work in the Resistance, I was able to get one of the first passes to return to Paris after the Liberation of the city at the end of August, 1944. I had at last received a message from my husband – he was alive! – saying that he had just returned to the capital where he had participated with the troops of General Leclerc for the liberation of the city. Ironically, Frédéric Joliot-Curie was there too, making the Molotov cocktails which were tossed with great effect by the insurgents in their battle against the German tanks. And so I left Brive and rushed north to home, to a free Paris, to find as fast as I could the loving arms of my husband, hero of my heart, whom I had not seen for four long years. The war was over and we were all safe!

Chapter 5
The *Sema*: The Sultan Valad Procession

The dervish is ready to flow

The *Peshrev* musical interlude now continues with the Sultan Valad Walk, performed in honor of Mevlana's son. It symbolizes man's identity and his place within a circle, and how the progress on the path to Truth and Reality can be realized only by trusting a guide who knows the way.

The Sheikh takes one step to the front of his post, bows his head, and begins to walk slowly around the *semahane*. He begins his walk with the right foot, pausing with the toes of the left foot behind, then brings the left foot next to the right and continues in this manner around the *semahane*, followed by all the dervishes. The dervishes, wearing black cloaks, circle the hall from right to left, the same counter-clockwise direction in which pilgrims circle the Kaaba in Mecca. The rhythm of the Sultan Valad cycle is called the "grand cycle" (*Devr-i Kebir*) and are the longest rhythmic sentences used in Mevlevi music.

The dervishes stop in pairs in front of the Sheikh's post and bow to each other in the *niyaz* position of humility. During the *niyaz* bow, the dervish places his right hand under his black cloak over his heart and his feet are crossed with his right big toe covering the left one. As they bow, they look between the eyebrows of the dervish opposite them and contemplate the divine manifestation within the soul of their brother. This gesture is known as *Mukabele* (to return and to act). The dervishes walk around the *semahane* three times, stopping to bow to each other at the

Sheikh's post. This walking cycle symbolizes the three stages of knowing: *ilm-al yaqin* (knowledge gained through study), *aynel yaqin* (knowledge gained by seeing oneself) and *haq-al yaqin* (knowledge gained through direct experience with God).

After circling the hall the third time, the last dervish bows to the post and returns to his place. The Sheikh takes his place at the red sheepskin *post* and the Sultan Valad Cycle ends.

Love is when a person introduces you to yourself for the first time. And that is what happened when I met you, Mevlana.

Paris was liberated from Nazi control at the end of August, 1944, and my little family was able to be reunited once again in our home. I returned to Paris after the war to find a whole new world had to be rebuilt. Not in stones, mind you, but in other ways; for Paris, unlike so many other blighted cities in France and Europe, had not been touched by the destruction of war. No, the Germans did not lay one finger on her magnificent churches and bridges, leaving her shimmering beauty intact. Yet so many people never returned to their homes and shops: soldiers, Jews, gypsies, merchants, homosexuals, the elderly and everyday citizens like me. We were the lucky ones, my little family; able to return from the Corrèze countryside safe and sound. Our apartment on the rue Claude Bernard had been occupied and all its furniture had been removed, its fixtures stripped and our paintings and keepsakes plundered, but bit by bit we were able to rebuild our lives once again.

I needed as well to rebuild my professional life, but how? I was 36 years old now and no longer a young student. The war had interrupted all my academic aspirations, it had changed my outlook, and, above all, I now had to take care of a family. To complicate matters, I was suffering from a tenacious anemia, a remnant of the war, and could not regain my strength. My husband was still finishing his studies and we did not have any money, not even enough to open a bank account! I was so weary, and my tired blood would not get better, but I worked hard, for I had no choice. My family needed to eat.

To reconstruct my existence, I continued to do translations of various articles and books to earn a living, but it was not enough. I decided to take the national civil service examination, for all France needed rebuilding and I thought perhaps I could be a part of that reconstruction. I passed the exam without a problem, most certainly due to my perfect English learned from my grandmother. I was appointed to a position at a governmental research and development think-tank founded in 1939 right before the War, known as the National Center for Scientific Research (CNRS). Its mission was to carry out of research to advance knowledge and to bring social, cultural, and economic benefits for society in all the various scientific disciplines. To this day, it is considered the world's leading producer of knowledge, so you can imagine how excited and honored I was to become a part of this nascent intellectual adventure. I became the assistant director of the Social Sciences Division, and I worked there with absolute enthusiasm, for I saw enter my office each day the finest specialists in the domains of the new scientific areas of research: ethnography, sociology, epistemology, educational theory, geopolitics, and ecology.

As busy as I was with my fascinating position at the CNRS and my home life – a second son was given to us at this time – I still had not given up the desire to continue my academic studies and the impact of Plato on me remained strong. I decided to pursue a doctorate in Greek philosophy and to write my thesis on *"The Symbolic Language of Plato."* How could one ever err with the study of the Greeks and certainly of Plato?

Greek philosophy was both probing and rational to me, and it brought all my nagging questions on faith to the surface once again. After all that I had lived during the war, I still hungered for something that I could not identify. A lovely home, beautiful children, a supportive husband and an engaging job, and yet those questions still nagged me. I needed a structure of thought; I craved a philosophy of total existence, but alas, Plato was only a movement of thought. I needed more. I was desperately crying for help in those days, sitting in my office and feeling lost as I was searching for answers that were just not there. I didn't know where I was really going with my life or what I was doing. I was a director of research, but not a leader of my own destiny.

Then, one day, out of the *grisaille* gray Parisian skies, a *deus ex machina* of sunshine appeared. A friend with whom I had studied Sanskrit years ago at the University came to visit Paris. We had stayed in touch over the years, and he had become the rector of the University of Islamabad in Pakistan. He was a former student of Einstein and was in France looking for suppliers for laboratory equipment for his university. I had not seen him for 15 years, and was thrilled when he paid me a call in my office at the CNRS. At the end of our visit, he handed me a book in English written by an Indian intellectual, Muhammad Iqbal, entitled *The Reconstruction of Islamic Thought.* Since he knew that I had always been interested in comparative religions, he thought I might enjoy reading it.

I did not know this author or the book, and I had absolutely no interest in Pakistan or Islam, so I put the book aside on my desk where it soon became engulfed in a sea of papers. I was so busy those days! One hectic day months later, while moving aside a towering stack of documents on my desk to hunt for a file, the book dropped to the floor with a resounding thud. I stared down at it, picked it up, and yet something inside of me prodded me not just to put it back on the desk, but to open it and take a look at it. How did this completely forgotten book find its way to the top of the staggering pile of documents and papers on my desk that day? And what was it that made me open it on that busy day, instead of tossing it aside and continuing on with my pressing work deadline? I cannot say, yet something definitely pushed me to pick it up and open it.

This Muhammad Iqbal, a national hero in his own country, was unknown in Paris, and I certainly had never heard of him. I learned that he was the spiritual and philosophical inspiration for several million people in India in the 1930s. He was a giant of a man: a philosopher, professor, lawyer, poet, politician, and statesman. It was he who had the idea to partition India to create a new Muslim state, and indeed, in 1947, this Muslim state, Pakistan, was at last created. Unfortunately he did not live to see it, as he died in 1938. He wrote essays and poems in Urdu, English, and Persian. How could I have never heard of such a brilliant mind? I began to realize how little I still knew of other cultures: here I was, preparing a doctorate on Plato, and I had never read one Islamic philosopher. I felt somewhat ashamed.

This man was a universal thinker who could cite Nietzsche, Spinoza, Bergson, and Freud all in one breath; men who had spoken to me as well. Intrigued that a Muslim thinker could be inspired by the West, I read on. Iqbal said he owed much to the philosophers Hegel and especially to Goethe, who bemoaned that the West had become too materialistic. Iqbal thus called on the East to provide a message of hope to resuscitate spiritual values by underlining the need for cultivating empathy and dynamism above consumerism. He explained that an individual could never aspire to higher dimensions unless he learned the nature of spirituality. I was intrigued by his words. As I turned page after page, I began to wonder if the East could help this proud Western woman in her emotional and intellectual disarray.

Yet, it wasn't just his comprehensive view of Western thinkers and faith that attracted me in Iqbal. He spoke of the poets and philosophers of the East and of Islam, a religion and culture of which I knew nothing before I picked up his book. His work analyzed the multiplicity of theories that were present in Islam, discussing tradition and modernity, structure and tolerance, fundamentalism and extremism. Above all, he invited the Muslims of the world to completely rethink the system of Islam without breaking with the past. He expressed his desire to reconcile the principles of the Qur'an and the discoveries of modern science. I had no idea what Islam was, or if it needed any rethinking, but many of the subjects of which he spoke made much sense to me. He believed in man and his will to progress. He discussed the responsibility of man towards God. He placed the individual at the heart of life and put emphasis on the liberty of choice in front of God. He also discussed the meaning of prayer in Islam, Muslim culture, as well as other political, social, and religious issues. I was immediately drawn to the universal aspect of Islam that he described so brilliantly in his book – a universalism that I so wanted to believe in; this universalism that states that there is one truth, one belief, whether it is expressed in Chinese, Urdu, or Cyrillic letters. A universalism founded on the belief that everything is this world converges together as one existence, not one of war.

He discussed even more ideas, and for the first time I heard a new word: *Sufism*. He spoke in particular of his conviction that Sufism, the mystical dimension of Islam, activates the searching soul to a superior perception of life. I was particularly struck by his invention of a word in English he used to explain this: "*I-am-ness*," his belief in the affirmation of the individual and his potential to come to know Reality and absorb its divine attributes in himself. For Iqbal, the aim of life is self-realization and self-knowledge. We are all on the path to become the best we can be, to find our "I-am-ness" in our search for spirituality. Quite simply, he urged that it is our responsibility to be a human being at his finest. Building humanity is our task, and it is by becoming the best human possible that we will be able to create humanity together. He believed that we are thus responsible for our world, our ecology, our peace and our well-being, and that we must strive to become what Islam calls being a "Vice-Regent" of God on earth.

I devoured his words. After all the horror of the war and the concentration camps and the hatred among peoples, the idea that man needed to be a vice-regent of our humanity carried particular significance to me. I had no previous idea of the existence of these thoughts, and a wide window opened in my office that day, blowing a fresh wind of inspiration across my desk from the East. He made so much sense, and what he said spoke to me more directly than any philosophy text I had ever studied, even Plato. His thoughts and this Sufism of which he spoke seemed to promise the answer to the many questions concerning the ambiguous direction of my life. Once I closed the pages of that book, I knew my life would never be the same, and, furthermore, it spurred me to open another life-changing book: *your* book, Mevlana, the *Masnavi*.

Yes, it was there in the pages of Iqbal's book that I first met you, Mevlana. It was in that book by Iqbal that I first heard your name and read your verses. He mentioned you quite frequently in his book, citing you as the major influence in his life. Who in the world were you, I asked myself; who is this *"Rumi"* he called his "master-thinker"? You revealed yourself to Iqbal as his guide to spiritual development, as a symbol of the infinite quest for God by man. Iqbal said that the Qur'an and the *Masnavi,* your book of verse, were the two basic works for man's spiritual education and he advised all to read your *Masnavi* and to take inspiration from it. You, Mevlana, became for Iqbal the counter-weight against the forces of cold reason and dry philosophy. My ears perked up at all of this. Who were you, this man whom Iqbal discussed in the same breath as Nietzsche's concept of the Superman? Who were you and what was this book, the *Masnavi*?

I found you there in that book of Iqbal, in lines black and white, yes; but not ones of dry or cold philosophy, but rather ones of shining light and multicolored vibrancy. I read three of your poems that Iqbal included in his book and my head and heart spun. I read your words and it seemed as if a voice in my heart were dictating them: *"Everything started with the cry of a craving soul: nourish me for I am hungry and hurry, for time is a sword."* Here in three poems I had found a being with the intellect of Plato, the enlightened soul of Jesus, and yes, the colossal literary gifts of Shakespeare. How could it be that one person could have such philosophical lucidity and such supreme spirituality at the same time? Yet you did. Your passion, your gorgeous imagery and your honesty hit me directly in the heart, just as the words of Jesus struck his disciples and Paul.

Upon reading those few verses of yours, Mevlana, there was no turning back from the appeal of this authority of Divine Truth you revealed. I had to learn more about you and this Sufism you represented.

I ran to the library and tried to find more about you, but there were few books to be found, and certainly none in French. Here you were, Mevlana, one who had transformed the life of a man who in turn transformed the life of millions of Indian Muslims, and yet I could not find one book about you in the supposedly hallowed haven of Enlightenment values that is the French National Library! But I did find other books on Islam, and I began to read the key mystics and thinkers of Islam of which up until now I knew nothing, absolutely nothing. I read, as well, French books written on Islam and I could see that many of our Islamic scholars were full of all sorts of prejudices due to the fact that we were still living in a colonial era. But most of all, I tried to read all I could on Sufism, that word I had never heard of before Iqbal. I had much to learn about this inner mystical dimension of Islam, for I knew nothing about Islam, much less this specific part of it. I learned that for thousands of years, Sufism, or *tasawwuf* as it is called in Arabic, has offered a path on which one can progress toward the "great end" of Self-realization, the theme so present in Iqbal. I discovered that Sufism is a way of love, a way of devotion, and a way of knowledge; a way of life in which a deeper identity is discovered and lived. This was no "cult" of Islam, it was Islam in its purest sense; it is its beating heart. And there in all those texts, Mevlana, your name was mentioned first and foremost.

Sufi: such a beautiful word, so close to the French word "*souffle*," or breath. To pronounce those two syllables you must breathe outwards to the world. Indeed, Sufism is a breath; a breath of love over a world in sorry need of it. I began to inhale and exhale more deeply as I read on.

I learned that one who practices Sufism is called a *Sufi*, a *dervish* or a *faqir*. A Sufi is known as "a friend of God," and they call God "the Beloved." No one really knows where this word "Sufi" comes from. Perhaps it comes from the Persian word for the wool garment, the *suf*, the Sufi dervishes wear, or perhaps it comes from *safa*, which means purity. *Dervish* is a compound word derived from the Persian term *dar*, or door: thus it means one who is at the threshold between awareness of this world and awareness of the Divine.

Faqir is the Arabic word for a poor person. Why poor? It is because the heart of a dervish is poor of anything other than God. Sufis realize that they have nothing, that they are nothing without God. They rely on nothing in this world, only on God.

As I read more of the poets of Sufism that Iqbal mentioned in his texts – names that I, a supposedly educated and well-read woman, had never heard of – such as Shabestari, Attar, and Fahreddin Iraki – one thing stood out in all of their writings: their passionate love for God, their "Beloved." In the West, "Beloved" denotes the loved one of your couple; for the Sufis, it means God, or as they call it, the Absolute. I discovered that the aim of Sufism is to bring man on a path which leads him closer to God, a symbolic pilgrimage path they call the *tariqa*. A path of breaths, thus, with each breath longing to restore this unity of being the Sufis calls the *tawhid*. This search must be done by each individual in his own way, in his own heart. Sufis seek to remove all the veils between the individual and God. This journey begins with the faithful observance of the outer forms of religious practice of Islam, the *sharia*, the ethical law which guarantees individual rights and ethical relations between people. Without the outer practice of the moral principles as set forth in the teachings of the Holy Qur'an and Muhammad, there can be no inner practice of Sufism. Those who persevere on the path to *tawhid* arrive at the truth, or *haqiqa*, the direct experience of the presence of God. And over and beyond that, a small number of those on the path of breaths arrive at the ultimate gnosis, the *marifa*, an ongoing state of attunement with God and with truth. This is the station of the prophets and the holy sages and saints, and includes not only Muslim Sufis, but all the prophets such as Moses and Jesus.

But what did all these words in languages I did not know and ideas far from Plato and the Bible mean in my life, sitting here in my office while the gray Parisian drizzle covered the skies over the Seine? Yet I knew my heart covered with drizzle as well. I read on. I read your words, Mevlana, as you said: "*The path is the open road. The* sharia *represents the wider road, made for all men, while the* tariqa *is a narrow road, destined for the small number of those who want to accomplish the realization of their full stature as a Universal Man, the Perfect Man,*" the accomplished man who helps other men reach their potential. In reading you, I discovered that Sufism was not a bound religion, like the Catholicism of the *bonnes soeurs*, but one that was open, on both a wide and narrow path; and that I would be able to go at my pace on this journey. I discovered that I could strive to attain perfection, just as Jesus said, *"Be ye perfect, even as your Lord in heaven is perfect."* I realized that by becoming united with God, I would be able to help bring humanity, divided into so many sections after this horrible war, closer together into a deeper understanding of life. On this path I would be able to acknowledge the divine in every being and creation on earth, from atoms to ants to elephants to the oceans. Once I became more aware of myself, I could become a part of community of life and could serve that community. By letting go of my petty concerns, I would realize that love truly is the basis of all, just as the message of Jesus had taught me for so long. Love is the only thing which is eternal. I would realize that there is an aspect of truth in all religions; mine and this one and all the others, for love must be the path of the heart of man, the only path. In the bewilderment of all these new words and ideas, I established my own definition for Sufism: *"One who is purified by love and is covered in the warm wool cloak of the love of God and has renounced all else, is a Sufi."*

Could this Sufism be the path I have been seeking for so long? In any case, one thing was certain: nothing would be the same for me after reading those first three poems of yours, Mevlana. You would now become a central part of my life. I decided then and there that I would translate Iqbal's book into French, for I wanted to make sure that your verses could be discovered by others.

But most of all I wanted your light to shine on me and I wanted to feel the warmth of that cloak of wool upon my shoulders. I wanted the drizzle of doubt in my heart and life to lift. Iqbal wrote that you *"appeared in a vision and bade him arise and sing."* I, too, was now ready to sing. Yes, I would become a dervish ready to flow and trust a guide who knows the way: and that would be you, Mevlana, the one who would lead me to become one with God, poor, and rich at the same time. Suddenly the external form of my religion and my life paled before the internal quest you laid at my feet. I realized that, hand in hand with you, I had the potential to become something I had never imagined possible: a Perfect Woman.

And so I read on and on.

Chapter 6
The *Sema:* The Preparation to Turn and the 1st *Selam:* the *Sharia*

The dervish is ready to turn

The dervishes prepare to turn. They bow, and, in one motion, remove their *khirka* black cloaks, kiss them, and let them drop to the floor. In doing so, they show that they leave their worldly attachments in the grave and are ready to turn for God. They return to their places and stand arms crossed right over left, fingers stretched, right hand holding the left shoulder and left hand holding the right shoulder on their chests. Their feet are locked, right over left. This posture symbolizes the unity of God. They huddle together shoulder to shoulder, again, to show unity. The musicians play as the *semazenbashi* movement master approaches the Sheikh, both of them still dressed in their *khirkas.* He bows and kisses the right hand of the Sheikh to ask permission to begin the *sema*, and the Sheikh accords it by lightly kissing his *sikke.* He then steps away backwards to a position five feet from the red sheepskin pelt, in order to direct the *semazen* whirling dervishes.

The whirling is done in four separate parts called salutations (*selams*). Each section has a different musical rhythm and each represents a different path to Islam. The circle of the dance floor symbolizes the turning of the planets, stars, and earth around the sun. The first greeting, the *Sharia Selam*, is the esoteric path in eight or 14 beats. Here the dervish recognizes his birth in the world and acknowledges God as the Creator and his condition of servitude.

The Sheikh walks to the front of the red sheepskin *post* and bows his head. The dervishes also bow their heads. One by one, the dervishes approach the Sheikh, bow to him and kiss his right hand. He, in turn, kisses the dervish's tall, felt *sikke* headdress to give his permission to turn. After the kiss, each dervish begins to whirl, taking flight one by one, like birds in the dawn sky. The dervishes slowly unfold their arms and whirl as the Sheikh stands at his post, the musicians play and the chorus chants.

The dervish turns right to left, standing on the left foot and making a full 360 degree turn with the right. One foot stays anchored to the ground, while the other flies toward the aspiration to be united with God, the Beloved. After a while the dervish opens the right palm of his hand to the sky, and turns his left palm to face the ground. In doing this, he shows that he takes the divine truth and scatters it to the people. The energy from above enters through the right palm, passes through the body and then, from the left palm, into the earth. Their half-closed eyes gaze upon their left thumbs. Some dervishes stay in the middle of the *semahane* to turn, while others orbit around the rim. As the *semazens* turn, the *semazenbashi* movement master slowly walks among them, signaling with his eyes or the position of his white shoe to correct their speed or posture. The tall wool hats of the dervishes are pulled tightly over their ears and their heads are slightly declined to the right shoulder. As they turn, the lips of the dervishes move rhythmically as they softly invoke the name of God over and over again, repeating *"Allah, Allah."* The vibrations of their breath repeating this word fills the room and becomes the very air the dervishes inhale.

After about ten minutes the music stops and the dervishes complete a turn that will face them toward the Sheikh's post and halt. They lock their feet, turn their eyes upward without raising their heads, and close their eyes to prevent them from feeling dizziness. Then they quickly walk to the edge of the circle and stand lightly leaning on each other to prevent falling. As this first part finishes, the Sheikh comes to the front of the red sheepskin, lowers his head and inwardly recites this prayer: *"Oh you who whirl in the circle of love, Allah's blessings upon you! Allah's blessings be upon your feelings and your intentions. May He lead you to the truth, which is the beginning."*

You say: *"Look for the answer in the same place that you found the question. What you seek is seeking you."* And it was in your verses, Mevlana, where I knew I would find my answers.

After I read few verses of yours in the book of Iqbal, something happened in me – I felt a sense of hope; a beam of light. How could it be that reading three poems of yours, Mevlana, could turn my entire world upside down? But such was your powerful call to me.

I thought about Islam more and more, and I began to sense that what I had read in Iqbal – he, himself, inspired by you – could be the path I needed to pursue to resolve my spiritual anguish and to find the answers to my questions. But how could I even think of taking the path of this religion, so foreign to me? When I started to take my first steps towards understanding Islam after reading Iqbal, you can imagine that this whole idea seemed a bit preposterous. I was raised a Catholic and I had a Jewish husband. Even though I was ready for a change, all of this was not simple, especially at my age, for I knew one does not change one's religion like one changes his shirt. It was not by merely pronouncing the one required phrase, the *shahada*, that I would become a Muslim. I had too much respect for spiritual life to take this lightly. How would my two sons react to such an act? I began to think I was crazy in all this pursuit, but you kept calling, Mevlana.

What did I know about Islam? At this time in my life, Islam seemed so far-flung; it was an unspoken entity and a faith totally disregarded by the French society in which I lived. It was the religion of heathens, those North and Black Africans who lived in the underdeveloped colonies in Africa. It was the religion of cultures perceived as inferior by the West. My awareness of Islam went no deeper than the jet-black faces of the troops of African skirmishers, *tirailleurs, spahis,* and the *chasseurs d'Afrique* parading down the Champs-Elysées in their blindingly white canvas spats on Bastille Day, little semolina and almond pastries dripping in honey and mint tea, that new mosque not far from my apartment and the glorious colonies of the *outremer*...but that was all, and it was purely folklore. I had never met a Muslim in my life, nor had I visited a Muslim country. And here you were, showing me a civilization here as glittering as the ones represented by Voltaire, Dante, and

Shakespeare.

I tried to shut your words out of my mind. I hung on tightly to my Christian faith. I resisted. I did not want to break with the lessons learned from my religion of birth; I did not want to renounce my name, my engagement to secularism nor my belief in the equality of women and their important role in society. I was afraid. I was not ready to abandon Christianity and my known world, and yet I could not shake this growing interest in Islam. I began to think that perhaps I had not understood Christianity correctly, or that the *bonnes soeurs* with their pat responses of orthodoxy were not able to answer questions as demanding as mine. In order to devote myself to sorting out this overwhelming dilemma, I began a three-year study of Christian theology at the Sorbonne University to make sure that I was not just tempted to embrace Islam because I had misunderstood Christianity or was angry at it because it had not answered my questions. I wanted to be completely sure of myself, for I was scared to abandon my faith and wanted to give it every chance I could.

At the same time I was undergoing this intense period of personal investigation and the study of Christian exegesis at the University, I continued to read more and more about Islam. It was then that I came to discover the strong commonalities between the two faiths. These commonalities and the venerated regard held of Jesus by Islam and the Sufis in particular were considerable factors in easing my introduction to Islam. I learned that both Jesus and the Sufis taught the same: that love is the major goal of life. Jesus called all to awaken our slumbering inner dimension to find a new understanding of the Divine. He issued an invitation to a religion of the heart, and to enter into a personal dialog with God. Jesus taught us to let love and consideration for others grow, and to suppress the ego in front of others. The messages of the parables of Jesus were the same core of ideas I now read in your poems, Mevlana, for both of you based your worldview on the principle of love. Love is to see what is good and beautiful in everything; it is to learn from everything and to see the gifts of God in everything. It is to be thankful for all God's bounties. Love brings man to a deeper understanding of God, and the images in your tens of thousands of couplets attest to this. For you, love represents a force of energy that propels the universe and humanity. How could I not be drawn to the light your verses shed?

I now understood that the traditions of all faiths are saying the same thing in much the same way, despite their surface differences. And what they are all saying is the transcendent importance of compassion for others, as epitomized in the so-called Golden Rule, voiced by Jesus: *Do unto others as you would have others do unto you.* It is that simple. No complicated study of theology, philosophy, or comparative religion at the University was needed to understand that simple rule of life. All was there in the words of Jesus and in your verses, Mevlana, and the path you lit was now calling me to join it.

However, life at this moment threw me a challenge I never saw coming. My husband, son, and I had survived the war; we had survived starvation and the Nazis and the challenges of putting our lives back together after the war, but we did not survive fate. One afternoon, in a matter of seconds, my husband fell dead at my side from a heart attack. He leaned over, and I thought he was reaching out to play with the children, but he collapsed on the floor and was gone before I could rush over to touch him. My two boys thought he was playing a game, but this was no charade. My husband lay lifeless on the floor of our apartment, with the questioning eyes of my young boys upon him and my voice unable to make a noise. His sudden and unexpected death so soon after the end of the war left me bereft, with no defense against the future. I was now alone with two boys to raise and no permanent job other than my translation piece-work. This was worse than anything I had lived through during the war. I would sit desperate and terrified in my apartment on the rue Claude Bernard in the darkness after the children were put to bed and would cry; cry for the senselessness of the war, my husband's life cut short at such a young age, my fear for the survival of my children, my confusion and my fears for the future. My grief was overwhelming, and I was discouraged about everything. Yet I slowly began to understand that perhaps the mercy of God is hidden in the guise of wrath, as it was for Job. As long as I remained attached to myself, I would suffer through all the afflictions I met. In my grief, I turned to your words, Mevlana, and read: "*What is Sufism? – To find joy in the heart when afflictions come.*" I began to understand that perhaps this trial was a part of the path of my life, and, as difficult as it was to accept the fact that I had lost my husband, I still had two young boys and I needed to be strong, to keep moving forward on the path of life, no matter what.

The time had come for me to decide what to do with the rest of my life. I was 42 years old now: not old, but no longer a fresh and young woman. I was so isolated at home and in my spiritual quest, for the intellectual life of Paris certainly was not attuned to considering the relevance of such matters. This was the age of the existentialists, debating the despair of modern man in the smoke-filled cellars of cafés and jazz clubs of Saint-Germain-des-Prés. The writings of the existential philosophers, the darlings of the French intellectual world, constituted the new Gospel of the age. They stated that man is a hollow entity, full of despair, living lives with no meaning. Everyone listened to their words, which made so much sense in the era after the terrible war in which we tried to murder all that was good in our fellow man. Everyone was looking for sense in what had happened in those horrid years of destruction and death camps, and no one wanted to hear the word God mentioned, much less your verses about the potential of love, for the God of the "Daughter of the Catholic Church" of France had failed us all. How could I, an intellectual and educated woman, say that I believed that the answers to all our pain were to be found in something beyond us? I would be looked upon as a troglodyte from the Middle Ages, a valueless scientific in an increasingly modern world.

Sleep became impossible. I felt so lost and alone without my husband, yet I suddenly realized that I did know someone who could toss me a life buoy in all of these roiled seas. I had a compassionate guide in the person of the eminent Islamic scholar Louis Massignon. Who better than he to understand my anguish and my dilemma? We had met at the CNRS, and out paths crossed again after I had started to investigate Islam at the same time I was studying Christian theology at the University. We traveled in like circles, for we both were working in the nascent area of social sciences, but he became more than an intellectual colleague; he became like a father to me, even calling me his *"petite fille."* He was a precious pole of support when my world collapsed after the death of my husband – he was actually the first person I called when my husband died – talking me through the darkness of my grief with his serene words of encouragement. His gentle kindness, brilliant erudition and unfailing support fed my body, my brain and my soul at a time when I was completely adrift. Massignon was regarded in France as one of the pre-eminent researchers in the domain of the

Arab world and Islam, and was well-known for his translations of Sufi poets, notably the 10th century Persian Hallaj, who was the subject of his doctoral thesis. He shared with me his vast and luminous insights into the Muslim faith and Sufism. Massignon had a fervent relationship with Islam, yet always remained a devout Christian. In fact, he himself was a convert to Catholicism after a spiritual experience in the desert near Baghdad in 1907 when he was captured while doing archeological research. Perhaps modern doctors would say it was the delirium of sunstroke or malaria, but he claims he encountered God there in those sands, who came to him in a divine appearance – a *"visitation from a Stranger,"* he said, that liberated him from his past captivity. He kept repeating to me how odd it was that he experienced God in a Muslim context and not in a Christian church, but it was his belief that God was free to reveal Himself when and how He wants. As a guest in an Arab home during his research mission, he also experienced the hospitality of Muslims and their deep spirituality, earning him enduring admiration for the practical way of life of the Islamic faith and setting him upon the intellectual path of his life's work. This tender soul from Brittany developed a lifelong association with Islam and believed that his mission was to pave the way for a positive esteem of Islam by the Catholic Church. He was intelligent, kind, and very hard-working, and became the model of the intellectual I aspired to become.

On many evenings he invited me to his home, just a few *métro* stops from mine, to attend the *soirées* of the intellectual *salon* he had created. There I met some of the leading writers, archeologists, and intellectuals of the age who were sympathetic to Islam: the journalist François Nourissier, the sociologist Jacques Berque, Nobel winning novelist François Mauriac, the philosopher Henry Corbin, the historian Louis Gardet, the Catholic philosopher Jacques Maritain, the Jesuit Cardinal Danielou and the explorer Théodore Monod. My head would spin when I would return home at night, their brilliance blazing in my eyes and ears.

Above all, Massignon taught me to approach Islam from the context of how it is perceived in the West. He held a wide vision of the world, which included disciplines as varied as sociology, archaeology, literature, and spirituality, and he taught me that I, too, must be multidimensional in my approach to the world. In this way, he would say, nodding to me with his gentle eyes, *ma petite fille*, you will be able to better create a more welcoming openness for Islam in the West. Massignon may have been a passionate Catholic, but he was also a fervent supporter of the dialogue of civilizations, especially between Islam and Christianity. He tried ceaselessly to establish common points in the three Abrahamic faiths of Judaism, Christianity, and Islam and to encourage an exchange between them. He would say: *"Judaism takes root in hope, Christianity is dedicated to charity and love, and Islam is the center of faith."* He was the one that taught me that these three religions build upon each other. He dedicated his life to bringing to the forefront the richness of Islamic culture, and it was then that I knew I wanted this rich life as well; the one of bridges of ideas, plurality, and tolerance. I wanted to help others, for I have encountered that Stranger in the desert as well.

Rest assured, Mevlana; I did not put you aside while I was attending my classes at the University, healing from my grief in widowhood, and leaning on Massignon. On the contrary, your words were the first and foremost beacon for me. I read your verses in their English translation done by R.A. Nicholson; a version I must admit I found stilted and without grace. As I read more about you, I realized that our paths through life were somewhat similar. While I was making my way towards life after the war, you, too, were in a period of upheaval and transition. You lost your beloved wife Gevher at this time. Yet life has a way of continuing its call, and after a period of mourning, you remarried with Kerra, a Christian who converted for you and who bore you two more sons and a daughter. Like me, you found happiness in a marriage with someone of another faith. After your return from your studies in Syria, you fully assumed your position as a teacher at your late father's medrese and became a respected scholar in your own right. You took to writing an even larger amount of poetry and prose in Persian, the official language of the cultured world at the Seljuk court in Konya. You may have well continued along that tranquil path of teaching and Friday sermons, just as I might have continued with my thesis on Greek philosophy, but destiny had other plans for you. Just as my life was changed when I picked up that book by Iqbal and discovered you, your life was dramatically altered when you unexpectedly met a wandering dervish named Shams-i Tabrizi on a street corner in Konya. On a late October day in 1244, only one year after the fateful battle when the Mongols seized control of Seljuk Turkey, this wandering dervish from Tabriz in Iran appeared out of nowhere and blew into Konya like an autumn leaf in the wind. Shams was called the *"parinda,"* the winged one, because he was constantly in transit on his wandering path, with no possessions except his patched black coat.

All was Mongol fire and smoke across the plains of Anatolia, and there in Konya, a fire of a different sort broke out, the one that the wandering mystic Shams lit in your soul. The name "Shams" means "the sun," and he burst into your life like the rays burning through the clouds. This dervish became your spiritual master, or as you called him, *"the light of the eye, the clarity of reason, the brightness of the soul and the enlightenment of the heart."* There is no doubt that the meeting with Shams on a street corner in Konya was the changing point of your life. Just what was the exact question Shams whispered into your ear on that street corner that shook you to the core? Only the two of you know, but whatever it was, it pulled you by its tail and spun you into an entirely different universe. This was no normal meeting; you both fell at each other's feet in a meeting of two forces, of two seas, of two souls in search of a friend full of mystery, grace, and spirit.

I understand that once the two of you met, you secluded yourselves together in a room and there a strong bond formed which took you away from your lessons, your teaching and those around you. Could such a thing be true? You preferred to spend all your days in deep conversation with this nomad who had literally come into your life out of nowhere. With him you began to discover the depths of knowledge of the consciousness of God. For six months the two of you were inseparable, and you neglected your family, friends, and students who all complained that he had bewitched you. He threw boulders and thunderbolts of inspiration at you, and you became lost to this man; lost to the point where you forgot to eat and even drink water. All thought you were crazy, and, in many ways, I can begin to sense what overtook you. After a lifetime of studying and so many masters, you finally felt that you had found in Shams a perfect mirror to your own restless spirit. Shams was no mere spiritual grifter: he had a solid Islamic education and had memorized the Qur'an. Like you, he was a devoted follower of the example of the Prophet Muhammad. He was some 60 years old and you were 37, yet can it be said who was the master and who was the student? You saw in him a conduit to the God, the Beloved, and he saw in you a Master and the hidden saint he had long searched for on his wandering path.

Through your friendship with Shams you discovered love as the dynamic force of the universe. You and Shams realized together that *"knowledge is to cross from the unknown into the known."* Mevlana, perhaps you and I were both looking for a spiritual master – you found him and I found you – or maybe we weren't looking at all, but were open to meet one. Yet it is certain that when Shams came to Konya and I picked up that book on my desk of Iqbal and read your words therein, we knew nothing would ever be the same. Your life, my life, and all our work would become the echo of the blaze of that meeting with the sun of Shams; this crossing from the known to the unknown. He took you from your lethargic state as a plodding scholar and teacher and thrust you on a path towards God, ripping you from every ounce of your comfort. And that is exactly what you have done to me, Mevlana. The grey skies of Paris that I see from my window are now bright and full of his sun. Finished the perpetual drizzle; now comes a clear blue I never could have imagined seeing from my 5th floor window: it is the horizon of Love I now see above the Seine.

Yet, even though I wanted to turn towards that love and that light, and had received the support and blessing of Massignon, I was still afraid to take the radical step to change my religion and embrace Islam totally. I prayed at night for inspiration to guide me. *"Oh God! What am I to do? Oh God, can't you help me, can't you tell me what I should do! Send me a sign to help me!"* And God did send me that sign, in the form of a dream. Tossing and turning one night, I dreamt that I was dead and had been buried, yet at the same time I was still alive, able to see my tombstone, which was one unlike none other I had ever seen. On it was engraved Arabic or Persian letters – I did not know the difference between them then – spelling out *"Hawwa,"* my name in Arabic. This seemed quite odd, and in my half-sleep, I said to myself, *"This is strange, for you are not dead!"* and even wiggled my toes to make sure of that. Yet when I woke, I knew what that dream was trying to tell me. Yes, I had asked for a sign and I received one: I would be buried as a Muslim.

That dream was the final signpost. I had studied Freud at length, so I took the interpretation of this dream very seriously. I could now understand that accepting Islam was not a break with my past traditions. I had come to understand that no matter what the religion, the aim is the same: to find the internal dimension of our beings, masked by the powerful ego, to give birth to the dimension of love that is in all of us. I came to understand that Islam recognizes all the spiritual communities before it, and all their prophets and all the Holy Books: the Torah brought to Moses, the Psalms of David, the Gospels inspired by Jesus. The Muslim faith does not demand that we forsake our religion of origin because it recognizes all religions. Jesus could still live in my heart at the same time as Muhammad. Accepting Islam now appeared to me to be the natural development of the spiritual quest that occupied my thoughts since my days with the *bonnes sœurs*, the philosophy of Plato and my desire to participate fully in a spiritual life. Above all, I understood that you don't "convert" to Islam, you embrace it, for this religion contains all the others within it.

After that dream, I was now ready to accept this embrace. You called me, Mevlana, and I answered your invitation. You say: *"The universe is not outside you. Look inside yourself; everything that you want, you already are."* I looked inside of myself and understood that I was not leaving something, I was going forward. It did not happen overnight, with one radical or illuminated event; no, the path that led to the fork in the road was one on which I had been travelling for a long time. Its ground was soft to my steps, with each fellow traveler on the road, with each page turned, with each prayer uttered, with each discussion held – all kept urging me down the road that led to the fork. I was now ready to drop the black cloak of all my worldly attachments and begin to turn into a new path of life. I was now ready to pronounce the *shahada*, the testimony of the acceptance of Islam, and become a part of the *umma*, the immense assembly of Muslim believers. I knew through the initial discovery of Iqbal, the help and inspiration of Massignon and your inspiring verses, Mevlana, that this was the right decision for me, no matter how difficult it was going to be for my family, colleagues, and French society to accept. And so, in the holy year of 1954, at the age of 45, I knelt down and quietly pronounced the words of the *shahada*: *"There is no god but God, and Muhammad is the messenger of God,"* and became a Muslim. A new door to the rest of my life opened in front of me, and I stepped through it.

Chapter 7
The *Sema*: The 2nd *Selam*: the *Tariqa*

The dervish is ready to praise

At the beginning of the Second Salutation, the dervishes again pass one by one in front of the Sheikh as in the First Salutation. This time, however, they begin to turn without kissing the Sheikh's hand.

The 9-beat rhythmic pattern of this *selam*, the *evfer*, is somewhat slower, and the change of rhythm compels the dervish to contemplation. This salutation symbolizes the inner path of Sufism, the *tariqa*, the state of awesome wonder in the presence of God's might and the harmony of creation.

At the conclusion of this *selam* the Sheikh recites inwardly: "*O walkers on the path of love, may Allah give you total blessings and lift the veil from the eyes of your essence so that you see the secret of the center of the circle.*" Praise be to the Beloved!

You say: *"What God whispered to the rose caused it to bloom in beauty. He said it as well to my heart and made it one hundred times more beautiful."*

Mevlana, you have whispered to me and now I am on that path of roses.

After pronouncing that one sentence of the *shahada*, my life changed, but it was not a drastic, overnight transformation. The discovery of Islam came to me as if I were finding my true self, a return to the state of purity we all know at birth and which we hope to find again, just as Plato described in his works or as you did, Mevlana, with the image of the moaning reed at the beginning of your *Masnavi.*

My life did change in small ways after I adopted Islam. I learned the *Fatiha* chapter by heart, the prayer that I would soon be reciting many times each day. I learned the movements of Islamic prayer, and how to wash before each prayer. I prayed five times each day, and came to understand that prayer was truly a meeting with yourself, not just with words. I learned what foods I should no longer be eating and I fasted during the holy month of Ramadan. I became calmer. I became accustomed to my Islamic name which was *Hawwa*, the exact translation in the Qur'an of my Christian name. I was still called Eva by family, colleagues, and friends in France, but Muslims began to address me as Hawwa and this other identity began to establish itself. However, I was too much a daughter of the Enlightenment to wear a headscarf which I consider an invention of the 20th century. I saw no need for a woman to cover herself before her God much less her fellow man. My purity needed to be read in my heart, not on my head.

Adopting Islam meant that I was able to take the path towards living the Sufi life. What exactly did that mean in my day-to-day life? It meant that I was to strive to empty my heart of petty concerns, to be of service to people, to let go of my ego, to practice tolerance, to seek personal development through discipline and responsibility and to worship God above all. It was that simple and that complicated at the same time.

I can't lie to you and say that this transformation in my life was easy: many of my friends – even my family – were unsettled by what I had done and shunned me, which was hurtful. It was not easy to suffer rejection from the circle of your loved ones, but it certainly tests the strength of your convictions. I felt isolated from everything at first, yet I knew I had done something that was meant to bring out the best in me. While my adoption of Islam symbolized the beginning of a new life and fresh opportunities for me, the community interpreted this act as a religious and political betrayal. Few made the effort to try to understand the motivations behind my acceptance of this new faith, except of course, dear Massignon, who stood by my side through it all. Could they not see that I had not broken entirely from the road traveled up to that point? I sought only to enhance the faith of my birth by accepting a further growth. Did not Jesus himself say: *"I did not come to abolish but to accomplish"*?

I soon realized that a new family of supporters would replace the naysayers, for I was now a part of the *umma*, the community of believers of Islam. I saw that one could be part of a fraternal cosmos reflected on earth in a community which goes beyond all borders, countries, and languages, for one is brother to a Muslim before one belongs to a specific nationality; one is Muslim first, and then a brother to all men on earth. After the horrors of the war that my supposed Europe of the Enlightenment had lived, this thought was one I needed to believe. How ironic, too, that my apartment on the rue Claude Bernard should be such a short walk from the Great Mosque of Paris! I started to go there for prayers, tentatively at first, but soon I walked under that wide archway shoulder to shoulder with black Africans, blue-eyed Kabyles and tawny Moroccans, yet never felt that this little white French woman was not accepted by any of them. It was at this time that I discovered, just as Massignon had done in the desert, that one of the utmost qualities of Muslims resides in their sense of hospitality, their generosity and their sense of graciousness towards all guests who are considered sent by God.

Was it bad timing or destiny that I should have chosen to become a Muslim in 1954, the year that another war broke out in France? The Algerian War of Independence was even more pernicious, I think, than World War II, since France was fighting amongst its own citizens. But had the French ever considered the Algerians as truly French? Were the same systems of justice, education, and health care in place in Algiers as they were in Paris for all citizens of the *République*? Was the same *égalité* truly in place for all under the waving *tricolore*? How was it admissible that a minority of European colonizers could deny the same human rights to the native Muslim population? I will stand aside of politics, but this war was an ugly one; with guerilla warfare, bombings, murders, *maquis* fighting, terrorism and counter-terrorism operations, killing, and torture on each side, both in Algeria and in France. Ignoble events took place that shook me to the core. It lasted eight long years, caused the downfall of the 4th Republic and the subsequent creation of the 5th Republic which brought Charles de Gaulle to power. It saw the exodus of almost a million *pied-noir* French Algerians emigrating overnight to France, as well as thousands of *harkis*, the Algerians sympathetic to French rule. France was in no way ready to accommodate this influx of refugees, and social tensions reached the boiling point. In addition, this Algerian War marked the end of France as a colonial power, and this was not easy for many proud Frenchmen to accept. As you can imagine, this was not a propitious time to make the decision to become a Muslim. Arabs were hated, pure and simple – *sale race! espèce de bougnoule! boukak basané!* – and I was ashamed to see my fellow citizens take this attitude. I was often insulted, but I took strength in this demanding journey of faith and political convictions from the ever-faithful support of Louis Massignon, who carried out hunger strikes and laid down in front of the first army tank leaving for Algeria. Such a man of principles, he was! I took solace in the fact that he saw the end of this war a few months before he died in 1962.

I suppose the most significant way in which my life changed after becoming a Muslim was that I now had a true direction in which I could pour not only all my spiritual quest but all my intellectual endeavors. I was in full middle age now and it was time that I started to achieve and create. I had a mission now, and it was clear: I would translate the books of Iqbal, this marvelous Indian Muslim mind, into French. I would continue to read you, Mevlana, and discover your work and Sufism. I would begin to write about Islam and share my insights with others in lectures and articles.

Shortly after becoming a Muslim, I finished the translation of the Iqbal book that had so changed my life. I had started on this project several years before, and, with the support of UNESCO, the translation of *Reconstruction of Religious Thought in Islam*, with a preface written by my dear friend and inspiration, Louis Massignon, was published. This book was my first gift to the Islamic community of France, and it opened a door for me to further a better awareness of this faith. It was also the first time that I signed my work *"Eva de Vitray-Meyerovitch."* I wanted to associate Vitray, the maiden name of my beloved grandmother, to that of my husband, for it was due to her that I learned the importance of being honest with myself, and that personal honesty led to this book being published. I decided to translate as many works of Iqbal as I could, including his thesis on Persian metaphysics, his poems, and his *Javed-Name*, a long poem addressed to his son, a bit like the Divine Comedy; only this time, it is you Mevlana, who served as his son's guide through the heavens, as Virgil did for Dante. In the end, I translated six books by Iqbal, and in doing so, I believe I repaid the debt I owed him for changing my life, for without him, I never would have met you.

My life was however not all dedicated to you, Mevlana. I continued to work at the CNRS, but at my request, in a less demanding position than I held before. I carried on as well doing my piecework translations in order to adequately support myself and my children. I was fortunate to receive a commission to write a book on Henry VIII from a publisher who knew of my knowledge and passion for English history. Although Henry VIII was not an admirable character in my eyes – such an evil man compared to you, Mevlana, soul of purity! – and one I certainly would not have chosen on my own, I was intrigued by all the fascinating historical characters in his sphere and I focused my attention on them. I also translated a book written on a magnificent woman born the same year as I, Simone Weil, the Jewish-born, Christian mystic and philosopher who perished tragically in the war.

My days were a whirlwind of activity, yet in all this flurry, I knew I still had one job above all others: I had to raise two young sons all by myself. I alone was responsible for the entire support of my family. My thoughts had to be of them first and to put food on the table to make strong bones and minds. How would I be able to educate them, to send them to the best schools and give them every opportunity in life? I was so lonely, so afraid, so overwhelmed by grief. I would sit at my work table at 4am, trying to put some paragraphs together before it was time for my sons to rise and I needed to prepare their breakfast and school bags, and then to comb my hair and get ready to head off to my office. But in these predawn hours you were always by my side, Mevlana, guiding my pen and giving me courage. I might have been terribly afraid, but I was not alone. You say: "*When you go through a hard period, when everything seems to oppose you, when you feel you cannot even bear one more minute, never give up. Because it is the time and place that the course will change.*" My husband

77

was dead, my bed was empty, but my heart was full. I tried to recall this bounty in the moments when the challenge all seemed so overwhelming. Two boys to raise by myself; yes, I could do this. I needed always to remember that I was a woman and a mother before I was a scholar. I needed always to remember that the most important job I had was to put soup on the table for my children. Day after day I peeled the carrots and chopped the onions to make the soup for my sons, just like an apprentice dervish in the *matbah-i sherif* kitchen of a Sufi lodge. I chopped and chopped and my problems with thorny translations dissolved in the bouillon, your verses swirled in my head as I stirred the bubbling broth and the steam of your inspiration reached my nostrils along with the aroma of the stock. Yes, I would earn enough from those translations and articles and lectures to buy the carrots to make the soup to raise strong sons. This is what I had to do above all else. And then I could bring the nourishment of your warm soup to others, Mevlana, as all the sons of the world are in such need of it.

I also made several professional decisions at this point of my life that completely broke with the past and launched me towards the future. The war, raising my two small boys and the death of my husband had put my academic life on hold for almost a decade, and it was now time to rethink what I wished to do with this part of my life. Once I had read your verses, a page had been turned and there was no hesitation on my part. I now began to study Arabic and Persian in earnest, for somewhere in the back of my mind, I knew that my ultimate goal would be not just to translate Iqbal into French, but to translate your verses as well, although I did not realize at the time what dimension that endeavor would entail. I knew it would take me several years before I would be competent enough in Persian to begin to translate your complex verses, but I faithfully dedicated a part of each day to learning this language, all the while I kept translating more books by Iqbal and working on other projects.

More importantly, I made the decision to abandon my doctoral thesis on Plato, who no longer held the same meaning for me since my discovery of your verses. Instead, I decided to do a thesis on the mystical aspects of your poetry. It was not easy for me to abandon the intellectual enquiry of the Greek philosophers to buy the marvel of God. Yet my soul was crying, craving for more than Socratic debate. I hungered for rapture; I wanted mystery. And behold, I knew those answers would be found in the very place I was looking: your verses. I was at the midpoint of my life; perhaps a bit old to take on such an endeavor, especially in these difficult times of the Algerian War, but I persisted. We were now bound together and my destiny was in your hands, Mevlana.

Switching from Plato to your verses, Mevlana, was actually not a rupture from Plato, for his philosophy exists everywhere in your work, which is a continuation of the exploration of unreal forms and the theme of reminiscence – *anamnesis* – that Plato developed in his dialogues.

I learned, Mevlana, through your images and fables that you believe that all we see is actually a veil over reality. The Prophet Muhammad said there are "70" or "70,000" veils of light and darkness separating man from God and the aim of Sufism is to eliminate those veils. This was exactly what Plato was trying to describe in his analogy of the cave, and I felt perfectly at ease with Sufism, which, like the philosophy of Plato, encourages contemplation and the understanding that there is an eternal reality far more complex than the ephemeral one in front of us.

Like Plato, you make a clear distinction between form and meaning: form is a thing's outward appearance, meaning its inward and unseen reality. A well-known saying of the Prophet says, *"I was a hidden treasure and wanted to be known, so I created man in order that I might be known."* God's love is found in every single object in the world, from the smallest atom to the stars in the skies. Mevlana, everywhere in your verses you describe God's loving signs which lead man to reflect upon signs of the attributes of God that are within him, and to play his own part in revealing this Hidden Treasure. Your Shams said it so beautifully as well: *"For those who can read, God has revealed His secrets in the Qur'an. For those who can see with the eyes of the heart, God has placed His treasure within His creation."*

An ornate Louis XIV-style gilded mirror has hung in the entryway to my Paris apartment for as long as I can remember, but now I do not look in it the same way as before. Each time I pass it, I now think of how you have shown me that man is a mirror; a mirror which reflects the cosmos of our existence. The visible world is a way to see the invisible: there is nothing in the visible world that is not a symbol, or a reflection in a mirror, of the realities of the invisible world. In this ephemeral life of ours, our task is to understand, or at least to feel, with all our being, that we are united in this universe, to God, and to all that exists, not only people, but animals, plants, and flowers. Gaze into the mirror and you will see more than yourself – you will see that treasure of all God's creations that Shams described. The essential basis of life is the belief in this Unity of Existence (*wahdat-e-wudjud*): we as one live in one world. Yet, the more we stay attached to our "little me" and not the "big us," we will remain forever captive of a world of separation. The only way to escape this divergence is to have a heart pure and polished like a mirror, for then you will realize that it is not your image you are seeing, but the image of the whole of humanity and all the living creatures of God's hidden Treasure. When I pass in front of that mirror now, I am reminded of this important lesson of the Sufis. Man must cleanse his heart, to ultimately transform it into a gleaming mirror reflecting God – much like the "*pure in heart*" of Jesus.

I also realized at this time that there was something which could bring your message to the forefront more vividly than any of my translations, articles, or lectures: the stately splendor of the *sema* ceremony. I felt that if people could see this noble prayer in motion, they would be moved to a more compassionate sensitivity to the beauty of Islam, Sufism, and your work. I desperately wanted to bring the whirling dervishes to Paris, but this was not an easy task. In 1924, with the end of the Ottoman Empire, the turning of the *sema* had been forbidden in public for over 25 years, although devoted dervishes continued to turn in private. Starting in the mid-'50s, a small group of dervishes convinced the local government of Konya that it would be beneficial to reintroduce the *sema* as a historical tradition to the new culture of Turkey, the one which wished to open to the West through tourism and trade. I knew a group of these Turkish dervishes, but I didn't know if they would come to Europe even if I could find the funding to bring them here. I approached my colleagues at UNESCO to get their support, and they wholeheartedly agreed to sponsor me in this initiative. Parisians watched in awe as nine *semazen* turned to the music of several dervish musicians at the Théâtre de la Ville on the Châtelet Square in the center of Paris in 1964, the first appearance ever of the whirling dervishes in Europe. Who could have imagined that the white robes of the dervishes would take flight in the very shadows of the towers of Notre Dame? It was one of the happiest evenings of my life, and I was right; this performance did attract much enthusiasm and many articles were written on the subject which stimulated the beginning of a widespread interest in your works in the West.

The time had come for me to take yet another significant step. Here I was, a devoted Muslim dedicated to bringing your message to the West, and I had never yet traveled to an Islamic country. The time had come to go east, and of course I chose your land, Turkey, to visit in priority. It would be the first of many trips I took to Turkey, destined to become a soul mate country for me. It is hard for me to describe that first visit to Istanbul; to see minarets instead of steeples, to hear *muezzin* calls instead of church bells, and it seemed a bit of a dream. People there called me *Hawwa Hanim*, "Lady Hawwa," and, thanks to the hospitable kindness of the Turks, I felt as if this were a true homecoming.

I was pleased to be reunited there with several of the whirling dervishes that I had brought to Paris two years before. One of them, an architect by profession – for all dervishes work and have family lives – took me to visit an ancient Ottoman dervish lodge in Istanbul that he was restoring as a museum. As we walked through the worksite I stepped over piles of gravel, heaps of broken stones and ironwork and I tried to picture what this dervish lodge must have looked like when it was built several centuries before. I turned my head and immediately my heart stopped, for there in front of me was the exact tombstone I had seen in the vision I dreamt right before my conversion to Islam, the dream of the tombstone with my name engraved on it which I had taken as a divine sign that I was to become a Muslim. My dervish architect friend explained to me that we were walking through the women's section of the *"hamushane,"* the "silent house" burial ground of the former dervishes of the lodge. You can imagine my emotion as I gazed upon this tombstone, an experience which made me all the more dedicated to the path you had laid out in front of me.

You, too, had a mirror hanging in the hallway of your life, a mirror in the person of that wandering dervish named Shams. Oh, your beloved Shams! The arrival of Shams was the upheaval in your existence, just as you have been in mine. He swooped down upon your soul and triggered a shift in your approach to piety and spirituality. You discovered that beyond the safe and traditional forms of obedience such as prayer, fasting, and applying the *sharia* law, there was another way to creatively celebrate your relationship with God. He dared you to see beyond your everyday existence, just as you dared me to go outside of my boundaries. Alas, all did not go smoothly for you, and you suffered separation and trial. After less than a year together, Shams left you, for he knew he was not liked by your entourage – your second wife Kerra and your son Alaeddin especially – and just disappeared from sight one day. Night fell over your heart when he left, and you began to spill out your pain in Persian poetry, so much more emotional than the Arabic poetry you had worked in up until then. You developed the habit of slowly turning in circles and waving your hands as you praised God and composed your poetry. Eventually, word came back to Konya that Shams had turned up in Damascus, and you sent your son Sultan Valad to Syria to fetch him back. In order to keep him close to you, you gave the hand of your adopted daughter, Kimia, to him in marriage, but she died suddenly soon after their marriage. Shams apparently mentioned on several occasions that he was one day going to disappear forever where no one could find him. And one night he did vanish for good, and no one ever knew what truly happened to him. Some say he was heartbroken after Kimia's death and left Konya to wander again; others said that he was a spy sent by the Mongols and had been called back; yet others said that he was murdered by those close to you – your son Alaeddin was suspected in particular – and his body dropped down a well. The only truth we know is that he was gone, as inexplicably as he had come. Yet he left you with an energy that was as strong as the intense sun of summer, and the rays of that sun still shine upon us.

You went to Syria yourself twice to search for him, but once you realized he was gone forever, you looked for him in yourself. Reflected in the sun of Shams, you became as shining as the full moon. With his disappearance, you learned that awareness of pain is a doorway to the path of love, just as I had experienced with the tragic death of my husband. Man must not flee suffering, but must welcome it knowing that it increases his love for its opposite, the joy and ecstasy of union with God. You may have been desolate after the departure of Shams, but your despair fueled a nuclear fusion of the sun of Sham to your poetry, and that explosive energy remains with us.

The power of that poetry sustained me for the many long years it took me learn Persian, raise my boys, carry out my work at the CNRS, do my translations, and complete my thesis. In June 1968, after ten years of work, I at last defended my doctoral thesis at the Sorbonne. By a strange twist of fate, it was not at all evident that I would be able to step in front of the jury. The date of my defense, scheduled months before, fell immediately on the heels of the volatile period of student riots and civil unrest in France during May, 1968, when the streets of Paris and the economic activity of the entire country were shut down due to a massive social revolution against capitalism, consumerism, and traditional values. I felt both out of sync and totally in sync with these events as I walked to the Sorbonne, whose doors had only days before been forcibly reopened by the police. As I stepped in front of the jury to defend my thesis, you were in an odd way next to me in Paris, for did you not fight for the total liberation of oppression of the soul, as those young students were doing with their marches, pitched paving stones and street barricades? My thesis, entitled *"Mystical Themes in the Work of Jelaleddin Rumi,"* was successfully accepted by the jury. I was fortunate that a leading editor in Paris decided to publish it in book form a few years later, which once again helped me to spread your word of beauty. I was no longer young at this point, yet somehow with this thesis in hand I felt as if my life was just beginning, much as those young students believed they were at the cusp of total social change when they held those paving stones in their fists. That spirit of potentiality inspired me as well, and I was now ready to enter the seventh decade of my life with a renewed dedication to my work of bringing you, Islam, and Sufism, to the forefront of intellectual debate.

Chapter 8
The *Sema*: The 3rd *Selam*: the *Marifa*

The dervish is ready to surrender

In the third salutation, the *Marifa Selam*, three different rhythms of gradually increasing tempos are employed: the *Devrikebir*, the *Aksak* and the *Yoruk*. The fastest part of the Mevlevi ceremony is the last part of the third *selam*. The bond between the *semazens* and the musicians here becomes complete.

The performance of this part presents the opportunity for the highest spiritual joys to be felt, as mystical feelings reach the summit and are transformed into ecstasy. This part portrays the level of *Haqiqa* (truth and reality), the Gnostic path of knowledge, in which the dervish dissolves into submission to God and sacrifices his intellect to love.

When they turn, each dervish tilts his head slightly differently and holds his arms at varying heights. All varieties of position and movement are accepted in the *sema*, as God accepts all His children in the universe. The dervishes move as if there were only one dervish moving, chant as if one dervish were chanting, and breathe as if just one dervish were breathing.

At the end of this *selam*, the Sheikh inwardly prays: *"O lovers, true ones, Allah's blessings upon you! Your circle is complete, your souls are cleansed. Allah has led you near to Him, to the true level of closeness."*

A hand reached out to mine and offered me a rose, and I took it.

You must accept the invitations of life. Islam has taught me that what life hands you is a part of the large plan of your destiny, traced by the will of God, and of this I am now certain. You speak often as well, Mevlana, of the idea of "becoming," and that life is a series of successive changes in a world in continual creation. You say: *"Lovely days do not come to you; you should walk to them."* I, too, now find myself on a path of perpetual becoming. This destiny, this path of roses we now share together has led me to a new destination and a new victory – the City of Victory, *al-Kahira*.

Cairo! You can imagine my astonishment when I was approached by the dean of the University of Al-Azhar in Cairo with an offer to teach at this prestigious institution. The CNRS agreed to accord me a leave of absence and my sons were now grown and at the university, so nothing was holding me back from the call of this new adventure to the City of Victory – except for the fact that I had no teaching experience and could not speak Arabic! Yet I looked forward to the challenge of learning both these skills. I was no longer a young woman, but not yet old – at 60 years old what are you, actually? – but I was not going to refuse this opportunity, despite the fact that I was a bit anxious to leave behind my apartment and my comfortable world in Paris. Yet, as Shams taught you, Mevlana, one must step out of the comfortable conventions of life.

It is hard for me to fathom that I had been invited to teach at this famous university; I, a convert to Islam, a foreigner and a woman to boot! It appears that I was the first Westerner appointed to teach here, but the university dean was a forward-thinking man who wished to open the minds of his students to other points of view and opinions, and he believed that I had the capacity to do this. All those years studying Greek philosophy had given me a unique perspective with which I could compare Western and Islamic thought. My studies of Sufism, and especially of your work, Mevlana, relatively unknown in Cairo at that time, would also give me additional strengths in the classroom.

The University of Al-Azhar, 300 years older than Oxford and 500 years older than the illustrious Sorbonne of my Paris, was founded in 970 as the main mosque and learning academy for the new city of Cairo, which had been established by the Fatimid rulers from North Africa. Although the Fatimids were swept from power 200 years later, this mosque and university remained the hub of the religious and political life of Egypt. The Sheikh of Al-Azhar is the foremost religious authority in the country and the university is, to this day, the most revered center for learning in the entire Sunni Islamic community, providing free education and board for Muslim students from all over the world. I taught my classes in a modern building not far from the mosque, but the Al-Azhar mosque remained the focal point of Islamic Cairo.

I adored living in Cairo. The Egyptians have a touching gentleness in everything that they do, from their speech, to their customs, and to their costumes. My days were filled at the same time with simple pleasures on the street, contemplative moments at home and complex challenges in the classroom. I felt close to Massignon here as well, for he had a particular love for the Arabic language and had lived in Cairo for many years. He used to speak to me with tender fondness of his days in Cairo, and encouraged me to go there, and now that I am living here, I share his affection.

How I loved the neighborhood of Khan al-Khalili around Al-Azhar! The medieval bazaar of Khan al-Khalili, one of the biggest in the Middle East, was jammed with hundreds of lanes selling everything from water pipes, brass, leather, wedding dresses, plastic furniture, toys, handicrafts, silks, and pungent-smelling spices. I would go to pray at the Mosque of Sayyidna al-Hussein, the holiest site in Cairo, said to contain the head of Hussein, the grandson of the Prophet. Afternoons were not complete without a mint tea at Fishawi's Coffee House, a charming spot crammed with small, copper-topped tables and walls lined with antique gilded mirrors. I would spend hours in the Egyptian Museum, founded in the mid-19th century by a compatriot, the Frenchman Auguste Mariette, and gaze in wonder at the golden artifacts from Tutankhamun's tomb. I actually preferred the calmer atmosphere of the Museum of Islamic Art, and it was here that I educated myself on the many beautiful objects, both secular and religious, produced in Egypt during the Fatimid, Ayyubid, and Ottoman periods and gained an appreciation for the order and precision of Islamic art. I would stroll in Zamalek, the residential district on the Nile, with its charming houseboats, and pause to admire the Gezira Palace which had been built for Empress Eugénie, the wife of Napoléon

III of France, when she attended the opening of the Suez Canal in 1869. I never tired of contemplating the mosques and medreses built during the Mamluk Period with their zigzag bi-colored carved stone surfaces, tall bulbed minarets and ribbed domes decorated with floral or geometric designs. I would buy *foul maddamma* beans from a street vendor, or stop at a lunch stand for my favorite dishes: *koshari*, the stew of rice, lentils, and macaroni, or the Aswan specialty of *molokiya*, a bitter green soup made from jute leaves. So many new words, customs, and foods to discover!

At home, life was gentle as well. I lodged with Egyptian friends in a room with a view over the Nile. I had now learned Persian well enough to start the immense undertaking of translating your work into French, Mevlana, and I took advantage of my time in Cairo to begin seriously translating your verses. I pushed my desk over to the window, and would translate your verses, a cool *karkade* hibiscus tea at my side, while watching the slow waters flow by; these waters of ancient Pharaohs and of Moses, still filled with the white sails of sedate, time-honored *feluccas*. That continuum of history and memory kept your verses flowing during my many hours of translation work. I knew somewhere deep inside of me, after reading those three poems of yours so many years ago in the book of Iqbal, that I would consecrate my life's efforts – for however many years it would take – to translate your universal message which carries the essential values of Christianity and Islam, and, without renouncing anything, transformed them into a dimension of fraternity and ecumenism.

Mind you, not all of Cairo was easy to accept: the dirt and the garbage took a bit of getting used to after the pristine gardens and squares of Paris. I will never forget my visit to the Birqash Camel Market where hundreds of camels are sold every morning. The haggling voices of the traders are deafening and the smell is truly awful! Linguistically I was challenged as well, but my spoken Arabic soon improved enough for me to have conversations with all. I lectured in English as I did not feel adequate enough to express complex philosophical questions in Arabic – this was Al-Azhar after all, the gold mark of the Arabic language in the entire Muslim world! I may not have understood Arabic when I first came here, but there was one word I learned immediately: "*Inshallah*" – "If it pleases God." There are no fresh melons today, *inshallah*, tomorrow there will be. The water has been cut off, *inshallah*, it will come back soon. My son will complete his education soon, *inshallah*, and so forth. I must have heard it 50 times a day, and at first I thought it was a dismissive shrugging off any commitment. How wrong I was on that viewpoint, however, and I now understand why Muslims repeat "*inshallah*" so often. The notion of the present moment of time is significant in Islam. I have come to appreciate that they view existence as made up of a bursting constellation of instants of time, not one of a long duration of linear time as it is seen in the West. The present instant is both the end of the past and the beginning of the future. Each second is a bridge of perpetuity, because it contains at the same time the permanence of being in the past and the period of being in the future. The instants of physical time which man ordinarily notes on his watch are but markers of this eternal instant, a hyphen between what has been and what will be. Islam has taught me that it is our responsibility to seize this instant of life we are living. Mevlana, you speak of this, too, in your verses, and now I understand you better when you say, "*In each moment, you die and you are reborn; at each moment the world is renewed by divine action.*" Yes, Mevlana, your poetry tries to capture the character of this irreplaceable moment that will never happen again, for each one of your couplets is a fugitive moment in time but also an eternal one. The notion of time became one of my favorite lecture topics at the university, and I never tired of debating its differences in the Muslim and European cultures.

Most importantly, I felt that I became a true Muslim in this city. For this reason above all, I would say that my years in Cairo were the happiest of my life. The opportunity to live here was a life-changing experience, because I was in direct contact for the first time with a Muslim society, and it allowed me to organize my day around the five calls to prayer. The closeted religious life I had lived in Paris was now a full-blown experience of faith lived as a priority. When I would hear the call to prayer, I would stop whatever I was doing and become immersed in the moment of communion with God. Furthermore, to spend the month of Ramadan together with an entire population fasting by your side gave me a strength I never believed possible. I truly became a part of the *umma*, the community of believers.

Cairo may have been a Muslim city, but it was also a teeming metropolis of many peoples and faiths. I would walk down the streets bustling with Arabs, Coptic Christians, Orthodox Greeks and Jews. There were dark Egyptians from the Sudanese south, blond Greek women dripping in jewels and the latest European fashions, and burnished *fellahs* in white *jellabias* from the country- side. The whole world was here in Cairo; much more so than in Paris it seemed, which I always thought was the most cosmopoli- tan city in the world. Why, all in one day I could speak with a Cop- tic man outside the Hanging Church, a Greek merchant in the Khan al-Khalili and a Jewish rabbi outside of the Ben Ezra Synagogue. Now, more than ever, immersed in this city of intense population and faiths, I came to realize that religion is something different than what was taught to me by the *bonnes soeurs*. It is as you say, Mevlana: it not stone convent walls, pews, steeples, or prayer rugs; it is not crosses, stars, or crescents. It is not creeds or rituals or books, although all of those paths, if properly approached, can open the door to true faith. You have shown me that true religion consists in loving God and all creation and experiencing a blissful feeling of joy at being connected with the entire world.

Yet, it was in the classroom that I lived my most excit- ing moments in Cairo. What a miraculous gift I have been given here: a new calling in life! In Cairo I became a teacher, a *murshid*, something I had never imagined possible. You and I now shared the same profession: I was Professor Hawwa at Al-Azhar in Cairo, you were Professor Mevlana in the Iplikçi Medrese in Konya, both called to teach and open minds. The astute Seljuk Sultan Alaeddin Keykubad invited many renowned teachers, such as your father Bahaeddin, to Konya to establish a cultural environment open to an ethical and mystical vision of Islam. Is this not the same thing that was done in my case, by inviting a woman and a foreigner to teach Western philosophy and its relationship with Islam to Mus- lims? In the classroom, I spent days of excitement and enthusiasm with my students. I often spoke of you to them, Mevlana, and I loved to see how their eyes grew wide upon hearing your words. I taught them comparative philosophy, and I believe, thanks to Plato and the other Greeks whom I had studied so long, that I was able to bring new dimensions to the lives of my students. I asked myself each day where I would find the strength to teach these young minds, but in this task I took inspiration from the teaching styles of both Plato and you. I would take a theme, such as time, mem- ory, or truth, and I would examine how it had been interpreted by Western, Eastern, and Islamic thought. I stimulated their criti-

cal thinking skills by asking questions, using the so-called probing question and answer Socratic Method, which was none other
than the very same method you used with pointed effect, Mevlana.
We had such animated discussions in the classroom! My job was to
uncover in each student what was already inside of him, as if they
were following their tracks in the snow. I also learned to teach with
stories and anecdotes, taking the lead of both Jesus and you. Jesus
taught with parables and symbolism and you with animal tales,
relating stories that led from the apparent to the hidden meaning,
from the visible to the unseen or from the sign to the signified,
as would say the structuralists then professing at the Collège de
France in Paris. You did not pronounce categorical judgments on
the principles of which you spoke. Rather, you let your students
the liberty to choose between diverse solutions – yet you certainly
knew how to adroitly guide them so that they would arrive at the
conclusion that seemed the most just! You wanted the student –
the *murid* – to discover, through your stories, discursive anecdotes
and verse, his own path – the Sufi path. How I loved to share with
my students your famous stories of the citadel with ten doors, the
dragon in the snow and the contest between the Chinese and the
Byzantine painters and watch their reactions!

I learned about your teaching style, not only by reading the
tales in the *Masnavi*, but also by reading your other books, notably the *Fihi ma Fihi*, which contains 71 of your lectures and courses
compiled by your students after your death – in the same way as
was done by the students of the Swiss linguist Saussure – and the
Majalis-i Saba, the collection of seven Friday sermons given by you
in Arabic and Persian to explain the Qur'an and the Hadith. What a
teaching style you had! These were certainly not dry lectures: you
peppered your sermons and writings with entertaining tales and
instructive anecdotes, all of which combined in a veritable fountain of themes bubbling in every possible direction. Your teaching
style was a bit chaotic, jumping all over the place, but you made
this decision to be scattershot. You did not present a philosophical
system, organized in form and content in a linear fashion. These
were not stories of dos and don'ts and certainly not the traditional
dogma like the catechism I learned with the *bonnes soeurs*. You considered doctrinal points of secondary importance to your principal
goal of touching the heart of the student and helping to transform
him into a lover of God and the Prophet in order to become the

finest possible person. You taught me much about the art of non-assertive teaching, as did my students themselves, many of whom have become lasting friends.

It was not just in the University where I was called upon to teach, and not just about philosophy. I lived some unexpected and rather revolutionary feminist teaching experiences in Cairo, such as the time I was asked by an *imam* to come to a mosque in Heliopolis after the Friday prayer. I had no idea why he wanted to meet with me, but when I arrived, I found a group of over 200 men assembled there waiting for me. Point-blank, the *imam* explained his reasoning for inviting me there. *"You see all these men here? Many of them are hostile to the idea that a woman has the right to be educated, and so I thought that if you could speak to them, as a Western woman, a university professor and a mother, about how you became a Muslim through what you had studied in school, well, perhaps, your story would help them understand the importance of education. So, would you tell them your story?"* I am not sure how many men went home that night after hearing my story convinced of the importance of women being educated, but I felt that perhaps I had erased some prejudices in their eyes. I was also once asked by the Grand Sheikh of Al-Azhar to teach the Egyptian female students more about their legal rights, which he believed would make them happier human beings. Such feminist activity at this time could only have been done by a Westerner, and I once again understood the wisdom of the university dean for inviting me to Cairo to teach.

I had now been a Muslim for almost 15 years, and the time had come for me to accomplish the most meaningful of the five pillars of the faith: a pilgrimage to Mecca, the holy site where Abraham came with his wife Hagar and son Ismail and built the first temple to a unique God. Mevlana, you had visited Mecca as a youth, and I went as a 62-year-old woman, but I am sure the feelings evoked by this visit were the same for both of us. I chose to perform the *Hajj* to Mecca and Medina in January, 1971, three years after coming to teach at Al-Azhar.

During the *Hajj*, you cross the sacred valley and abandon your past existence, the one of this world, to reach the Reality of the invisible world. The *Hajj* is a human odyssey to God. I experienced an astonishing communion with humanity when I was there, far deeper than the sense of solidarity that I felt when I fasted during the month of Ramadan in Cairo. I felt as if I were a blood cell cursing in a gigantic body, a bee in the hive of life, a star shining in a heavenly constellation or a grain of sand glittering on the strand of the ocean of the world. It was an astounding moment of collective consciousness, and there is absolutely no doubt about the potent fraternity of the physical and spiritual community of the *umma* when you have two million people next to you, turned to the same direction and praying in the same fashion.

Although it was the month of January, it was terribly hot in Mecca. I put on the *ihram*, the plain white cotton gown that all the pilgrims must wear, which makes everyone equal, a fundamental notion in Islam. There are no signs of being rich or poor at Mecca: no distinction of race, cast, frontiers, education, titles, or money in the bank, for each person, dressed in his flowing white *ihram*, becomes much like one of the innocent doves of the *"Povarello d'Assisi,"* Saint Francis, the animal-loving *faqir* saint of the Catholics. I circled the black cube of the Kaaba seven times, and prayed in the vast ring of supplicants surrounding it. Instead of all facing the same direction of the *qibla* as is usually done during prayer, the faithful pray facing each other – only during the *Hajj* in the immense circle around the Kaaba is this possible – and encounter for the first time in their lives the countenance of their brothers or sisters facing them in the mystical circle of prayer, this ring of perfection, or, as you call it Mevlana, *"the face without a face,"* where the faces of many reflect the unique face of God.

My most cherished part of the pilgrimage was the assembly at Arafat, a vast plain surrounded with hills where one prays from dawn to the setting of the sun. These hills are the color of burnt Sienna, yet they were so covered with people in their white *ihram* robes that they appeared as if covered with snowfall, and when the people left, it was as if the snow had begun to melt. Following my visit to Mecca, I completed this sacred pilgrimage by visiting the tomb of the Prophet in the mosque of Medina.

Upon my return to Cairo, I kept thinking of those galaxies of stars, the melting human snow and the doves of Saint Francis that I had seen on the *Hajj*. As much as the pilgrimage had moved me, I realized that my struggle to attain the divine was actually situated in the compass of the human heart of my daily life. As moving as this intense experience of the *Hajj* had been for me, I now understood that to be a Muslim meant above all believing in God and polishing your mirror to best reflect His Light. The rest is just ritual.

Such is perhaps the greatest lesson I have learned from you as well, Mevlana. When the light of Divine Love is awakened within us, our capacity for earthy love is ignited to the benefit of all around us. And what better way to show that love than by teaching! I taught at Al-Azhar, and you taught at the religious academy in the Iplikçi Medrese in Konya. The people who attended your lectures were serious university students, but also the general public and merchants hoping to learn more about the Qur'an to help them in to become better citizens and trades people. People then, as now, gravitated to the best speakers, which you must have been, what with all those stories and fables you told! Some listened and went home, potentially enriched like those 200 men I spoke to in Heliopolis, and others became your disciples and dedicated themselves to study with you.

At this time in your life, you realized that Shams had disappeared for good and was never going to return. Your time together was so short – not more than three years – but you were changed forever. Despite all those rumors about his reasons for vanishing, in many ways I think that he disappeared so that you would accept your responsibility to your students and disciples. He did this so that you would find your mystic union not with him, but within yourself, and to look for God's light within your heart instead of depending uniquely on the presence of another person. After the final disappearance of Shams, you were consumed by an extended period of grief and introspection. To assuage your pain, you poured out your soul in ecstatic odes in Persian, Arabic, and some Turkish about your friendship with Shams, and this collection of poems formed the basis of your book, the *Divan*, or *Discourses*. You dedicated these mystic poems to the memory of Shams, whose name appears at the end of each poem.

Life went on, but your teaching was now different and richer. After a period of several years of grief over the disappearance of Shams, you declared that he had reappeared to you in the form of the merchant Zarkub, one of your students. You put the humble, unschooled, but well-intentioned goldsmith in charge of training your disciples. It was a different type of relationship than the one you had with Shams; more muted perhaps than the nuclear fusion of his blazing sun, but this alliance helped you to resume your role as teacher and author and offered you resonance for your thoughts. Shams may have vanished from sight, but he did not disappear from your inspiration, and you, Mevlana, will not disappear from us. I translate the reflected light of Shams in each verse you wrote.

I learned many things in Cairo, but perhaps the most significant was that I loved to teach, and the best way to do that was to bring different viewpoints and methods to my teaching, just as you did. One thing I knew for certain now: my life would be dedicated to transmitting your message, via teaching, translations, and research, which I believe is the highest way in which I can serve God. Your spiritual guidance must be shared with as many people as possible, for you are the finest model of what a compassionate Muslim should be.

My life was now floating calmly and steadily like one of those white-sailed *feluccas* down the Nile: slowly, peacefully, and steadfastly advancing towards accomplishing that goal, surrendering to the flowing current of your verses and to the breeze of their inspiration.

Chapter 9
The *Sema*: The 4th *Selam*: the *Haqiqa*

The dervish is ready to serve

In the fourth and final salutation, the *Haqiqa Selam*, the path of union is slower, in nine beats. The previous ecstasy is reduced and the dervish, who became delirious during the faster beats of the third *selam*, now begins to concentrate again.

In contrast to the previous salutations, the dervishes whirl in the outer circle where they stand, without moving around the hall. In this most beautiful of the *selams*, the dervish attests that he will serve God. Now the dervish experiences the state called *fana fillah*, the highest degree in Islam. It designates the cessation of the ego and the joining in existence with Allah (*baqa billah).* The dervish sacrifices his mind to love in a complete submission to love and devotion to God.

At the end of this *selam*, the Sheikh walks to the center of the circle, called the *qutb*, and begins to slowly turn. He does not remove his black cloak. He represents the eternal sun and its rays with the planets spinning around it. His entry to the *sema* symbolizes that man must return to his function on earth, and each dervish will go home as a servant of God, of His Books, of His Prophets and of His creation.

When I returned to Paris from Cairo, I was more than ever dedicated to continuing on this path now strewn with your roses. I learned in Cairo that teaching gave me tremendous joy, and I was ready to serve you and God by teaching in any way I could – by lectures in the public sphere, lessons in the classroom, translations and publications, interviews on the radio, and with one-on-one discussions with famous people and neophytes alike. I was open to use any and all means possible, for I believed that the transmission of your universal message was truly urgent. Mevlana, the devotion you expressed towards your own teachers – the Prophet, your father, Burhaneddin, and others – turned you into the best of students and then the best of teachers. I hope I can become the same, for I now know that every Sufi is a priest, a preacher, a teacher and a pupil of every soul that he meets in the world.

I picked up my pen and there was no stopping me now; your light was in my ink and I sailed forth into the world with your message, and before I knew it, I began to make a name for you. Upon my return from Cairo, I dedicated myself to translating your works and those of the influential Sufi thinkers who gave insight to the spiritual path. Drop by drop into the vast ocean of understanding, each book allowed me to get deeper and deeper into Sufism and your philosophy.

The works I completed in Cairo were now published, and they were the first translations of your verses to appear in French. The first of your books that I translated was the *Mystical Odes*, the series of poems that you wrote celebrating the spiritual friendship you shared with Shams. I then published another book I had worked on in Cairo, the *Fihi ma Fihi*, the compilation of 71 of your lectures and courses. It is the most accessible of your texts, and was perhaps the one that shed the most light for me concerning your thought, and thus, it was a personal priority to see its words come to life in French. It was the first time it had been rendered accessible in a European language.

I also authored my own books as well, and the text I wrote about you, entitled *The Mystical and Poetry in Islam: Rumi and the Order of Whirling Dervishes*, published right before my return to France from Cairo, garnered substantial feedback from literary and poetical circles. Yet it was two other texts I wrote about you, *Rumi and Sufism,* and the *Anthology of Sufism,* which drew the attention of the general public to you. Many of my titles were translated into languages as diverse as Rumanian, English, Spanish, Bosnian, and Czech, and the modest *Rumi and Sufism* book I wrote circled the entire globe. I have met so many people over the years who have told me they knew my name because they had discovered you through this little text! Even more astonishing is that my books were translated into Turkish, making it possible for an entirely new generation of Turks in your own land to gain insight into your work. People all over the planet at last began to know your name and discovered that you were not just the master of the whirling dervishes, but an accomplished and elegant author of universal dimension.

I wrote other books on you and also on various aspects of Islam, such as a portrait of Mecca, inspired by my *Hajj* there, two translations of the writings of your father, Bahaeddin – again, the first time they appeared in a European language – as well as an anthology of Sufi fables and several comparative studies of Islam and Christianity.

Yet, it wasn't just books I wrote. I also published numerous articles in magazines and journals, which offered me a more accessible platform in which to expose the tenets of Islam and Sufism. I did interviews and wrote articles for mainstream venues such as the prestigious *Le Monde* newspaper and the *Magazine Littéraire,* as well as smaller journals, such as *Planète* and the Jesuit journal *Christus.* The article I wrote for the Jesuits on humility in Islam was the first time an article about Islam appeared in that publication dedicated to a better understanding of the spiritual values which link the disparate parts of humanity, an important endeavor for the Jesuits.

I knew that the key to presenting Islam and Sufism to the French was to connect it to the Western frame of thought, a lesson taught to me by Massignon. I would pull in references to thinkers of the Western tradition so that readers might better comprehend the parallels between the two systems of thought: Plato, of course, but also St. Augustine, Rimbaud, Pascal, Jesus, Planck, Bohr, Zenon, St. Francis, Massignon, Bergson, Leibniz, Fenelon, Joubert, and Nietzsche. Many of the prominent thinkers of Western thought found their reflection in the spirituality of Islam, and, above all, in

Sufism, which encouraged people to see that wisdom comes from the same source.

It was at this time I took on the major writing challenge of my lifetime: I began to translate the 51,000 verses of the *Masnavi*, your major work. This goal had been bubbling inside of me for many years, and now that I had learned enough Persian and had translated your other works which led up to this one, your final work, I felt that the time had come to accept this challenge. This would be the most significant gift I could give to you, to the Islamic community and to the Western world. Your *Masnavi* constitutes a return to the pure essence of the Qur'anic revelation, yet, at the same time, it is an opening into unexplored dimensions. The beauty and expressiveness of your language, heightened by your insight into the universal values of love, was a gate into understanding metaphysical truths of the highest order: what more noble message could be shared with the people of our times?

The French were becoming more and more aware of Sufism through the lectures and radio and television programs I gave, and now Sufism reached yet another venue: the theater. The brilliant English director Peter Brook staged a performance of the *Conference of the Birds* by the Sufi poet Farid al-Din Attar for the celebrated Avignon Theater Festival in 1979 and the show came afterwards to the Théâtre des Bouffes du Nord in Paris, where it met with acclaim.

Legend has it that you met Attar in Nishapur, when your family was fleeing the Mongols. It is said that he gave you a copy of his *Book of Secrets* and predicted that you would go on to greatness. Whether you really met him as a child or not is perhaps not crucial; what matters is that later on, Attar became for you an influential guide on the path of the Absolute. You state, with reverence of this author: *"All I have said about the Truth, I have learned from Attar"* and *"Attar has roamed through the seven cities of Love, while we have barely turned down the first street."*

Three years previously, I had written the preface to a translation of Attar's *Memorial of the Saints*, which relates the lives of famous Sufis and their miraculous deeds, so I was quite eager to see this theater adaptation of the *Conference of the Birds*, the most important work of Attar. The *Conference* is a poetic allegory of the metaphysical quest for God, told in 4,500 rhyming couplets. I sat in the front row, transfixed by the emotions evoked by the beauty of the costumes, sounds, and exotic Balinese dances which Brook used to illustrate the travails of each different bird on his journey. Theater, with its particular form of magic, often opens a path to the most subtle and hidden layers of the human experience. This staging of the most famous Sufi parable had done just that. Indeed, all the philosophy of Sufism can be found in this story of a group of birds that set out in search of their king.

Although the birds had a zealous desire to meet the King-bird Simurgh at the top of the mountain where he lived and were enthusiastic to begin the expedition, they did not realize all that was entailed. As they progressed, it became apparent that each one possessed a fault which prevented him from completing the journey and attaining enlightenment. One by one, they began to drop out of the journey, each offering an excuse. Of the hundreds of birds that initially set out on the voyage, only thirty birds reach the abode of the Kingbird Simurgh. However, to their surprise, when they arrived, there was no Simurgh to be found, and all they discover is a lake in which they see their own reflection. The birds come to comprehend that they do not really exist as individuals, and then dissolve as drops of water into an immense lake of peace.

This fable of the birds illustrates beautifully the Sufi concept of annihilation of the ego, which they call *fana*. Sufis refer to the animal and carnal ego in each of us by the term *nafs*. This is the dark part of man which incites him to evil and keeps him from uniting with God – those nasty habits of the seven deadly sins the *bonnes soeurs* incessantly drilled into me. The true goal of the dervish on the Sufi path is to eliminate the veil of bad habits of existence and the pride of ego. Until the veil is lifted, man will remain in ignorance and error. You must strip yourself of pride, greed, lust, envy, anger, avarice, and hatred like a *"child who must wash his black slate clean before writing his letters,"* as you say. Once free of the things which hide the spirit from itself, you will be able to find, in your own depths, the spirit of the Divine essence hidden within you. Man struggles against the destructive power of these *nafs* relentlessly, day by day, moment by moment. Some win the battle, others do not.

The Kingbird Simurgh in Attar's story symbolizes God and He is in the deepest part of us, where we must go to find him. And when we find Him, there is nothing else, nothing left. This *fana*, or annihilation of the ego, forms one of the main topics in your

Masnavi, and I am sure you were inspired by this tale of the birds by your master Attar. You frequently use the image of death when speaking of the annihilation of the *nafs*, saying *"Die before you die!"* We must spiritually die to the person we have been conditioned to think we are, so that we might be liberated to become what we are capable of becoming, and fulfill the sacred trust that we must serve as the vice-regent of God on earth. Just like those birds, or like me, climbing up my stairs each day to my apartment.

There are 80 steps leading up to my 5th floor apartment on the rue Claude Bernard. I think of your words every night as I come home from work and trudge up those steps, my heavy bags of carrots and onions and books in tow. That climb is never easy and I am always out of breath when I reach my floor. Yet, to get home, the home of the Absolute, we must climb the interior staircase of our lives, step by step. You say: *"God has set a ladder before our feet which we have a responsibility to climb if we wish to reach the roof."* Others before and after you have spoken of this ascent of the ladder of Being, whose rungs of increasing awareness you call *maqamat*. Plato in the *Banquet* reminds us that the ascension toward contemplation, the *theoria*, can be done only in stages, or degrees, like climbing the steps of a ladder or floor after floor. The angels climbed Jacob's ladder to heaven in the Old Testament of the Bible. Mevlana, you say, *"Man ascends towards himself, from the exterior, which is darkness, to the interior, which is the universe of light, and from the interior to the Creator."* The ultimate goal of the Sufi's search is this spiritual experience, much like the Prophet Muhammad when he crossed the skies and made the *Miraj* nocturnal journey. Such is the Sufi path, taken one step at a time.

And what a glorious journey it is! I have met such interesting people on the path to make you better known! I understood that I needed to do more than just translate the texts of the leading Sufis of the past: I also needed to visit with living representatives of the Sufi path. I collaborated with UNESCO on several projects where I had the opportunity to meet the writer and ethnologist Amadou Hampâté Bâ. He was the ambassador of Mali at UNESCO at the same time he served as the sheikh of the largest Sufi lodge in sub-Saharan Africa. Such a gentle and wise man he was, with piercing blue-grey eyes, a noble black face and a heart as luminous as the full moon. Perhaps the richest association I had was with the Franco-Afghan Nadjm oud-dîn Bammate, with whom I worked to create a series of programs on Islam for the national radio channel, France Culture. He was an intellectual and Islamic scholar of the highest order, and spent much time writing about the need for the evolution of Islam in concert with the evolving humanity of the modern world, much as Iqbal had urged. We had many things in common: he had studied the law, taught at the University of Paris at Jussieu where I had recently been appointed as a director of research and he was a former student of Massignon, who communicated to him as he did to me on the need for a universal approach to faith. He did much to spread a high, open, and balanced view of Islam, and it was an honor to collaborate with him.

In addition to these radio and television programs, I tried to find as many novel ways as possible to bring our traditions together, and Jesus provided one of them. I may be a Muslim now, but my heart still beats faster at the approach of the Christmas season. A Prophet is born! Nowhere else in the world is this season celebrated with more festivity than in France, daughter of the Catholic Church. The roasting chestnuts, the preparation for the midnight feasts, the ringing bells of Notre Dame, the *crèches* in churches, the expectant eyes of children in front of the glittering shop windows, the delicacies on the market stalls, the *bûche de Noël* cakes lined up in bakery windows, the garlands of lights strung along the streets, midnight candlelit mass, the wrapping of gifts: all these traditions take me back to my childhood and my unending love of Jesus; yes, the savior whom I have never ceased to love with all my heart. God sends us gifts too, in the form of prophets, and Jesus, Muhammad, and the Buddha are some of the most precious of His gifts. God may have touched those prophets with his finger to make them one with God and themselves, but I believe we all have the potential to become the best we can be. For me, this is the symbolism of the gift of Christmas: we all have the capacity to become prophets in our own daily way. I searched for a meaningful way to organize a special Christmas event which would have meaning for all believers. I came up with an idea and managed to convince the nuns and priests of the Church of Saint-Germain-l'Auxerrois across from the Louvre to host an unconventional type of Christmas service, and, although it may have seemed a bit radical to them, they agreed to it.

I invited a *hafiz*, a man who had memorized the Qur'an by heart, to recite the Maryam Surat, named after Mary, mother of

Jesus, as well as the passages which spoke of Jesus in the Qur'an. Afterwards, the nuns read the Christmas story as it is related in the gospels of Matthew and Luke of the Bible. I invited many of my friends, Muslim, Christian, and non-believer alike to attend. I dedicated the mass to Louis Massignon, as he was the inspiration for me to create bridges among communities of believers. There, among the flames of the burning candles on that cold December evening, the warmth and the light of the words of two holy books wove together in a prayer to the spirit of Jesus and his love for mankind. The universalism of that message left no one unmoved.

It was not just at home in Paris that I gave lectures, but now the world became my stage. After my experience in Cairo, I developed a taste for travel and the wanderlust never left me. At the same time as I was writing and translating books, I traveled to the Middle East to lecture. I took on numerous speaking engagements to places as diverse as Libya, the Sudan, Kuwait, Pakistan, Tunisia, Spain, Saudi Arabia, and, again, to Egypt. I went to Pakistan as a guest of the son of Iqbal, who gave full blessings for my project to translate as many works as possible of his father's into French. I discovered North Africa, the *Maghreb*, at this time as well, and I went at least 15 times to both Algeria and Morocco. Both were delightful discoveries for me, as much for the beauty of the countryside as for the hospitality shown me by the people of North Africa. It was a moving moment and a meaningful internal connection for my spiritual life when I prayed with a group of Algerians who had several years previously bitterly fought my countrymen to win independence for their country. In all these countries, I was called to give lectures on different topics concerning Islam and Sufism, where, as at Al-Azhar, I would compare themes in Western philosophy and Islamic thought.

One voyage stood out among them all: Iran. I admired the refinement with which the Iranians lived, and the splendor of their art and architecture. My visit to Iran, which took place during the time of the Shah before he fell from power in 1979, was of utmost significance for me for another reason: it was there that I met Jamshid Morazavi, the former dean of Tabriz University. We shared the same admiration for your work, and he accepted my invitation to assist me in the translation of your *Masnavi*. I knew that I could not face such an undertaking alone, so I was thrilled to have his support. There was no stopping now; my goal of bringing to life this major piece of world literature was now launched and there would be no return.

Yet, there was one destination I held in esteem above all others: your city, the holy city of Konya. In Konya I discovered that I was not alone in my veneration of you, for this city lives and breathes the wonder of your legacy. Here you are revered as a saint; your odes and quatrains are learned by heart, your stories are given as moral lessons, and your thoughts are endlessly quoted and commented upon. I visited Konya for the first time during my years at Al-Azhar, and an inexplicable magic overtook me as I walked down the streets of this city. Was it your words I heard on the wind, or was it the echo of the prayers of the thousands who came to visit your tomb, or perhaps was it the soft shuffle of the leather shoes the dervishes wear when they turned in the *sema*? I cannot know, but it is certain that there is a supernatural aura in Konya.

Konya! Prehistoric city near the 9,000-year-old Neolithic-era village of Çatalhöyük, considered the world's oldest settlement. Konya, cradle city of the Hittites, located at a cross-road where the paths of caravans and meditative mystics intersected. Konya, city of Christianity, which welcomed Saint Paul, the most fervent disciple of Jesus, and became the first city he evangelized. Konya, crown city of the Seljuks, which reached its apogee in the 13th century in an exceptional climate of open exchange among the diverse religious beliefs of Christians, Jews, and Muslims. Konya, city of Sufism, where your father settled and where you chose to remain your entire life and establish the fraternity of the whirling dervishes. Konya, noble city of traditions and folklore, densely sweet halva, robust Seljuk food, intense rainstorms in May that turn the entire plains green, and colorful red woolen carpets covered with sparkling yellow stars.

When I am in Konya I think often of your funeral, attended by the Jews, Christians, and Muslims alike, and try to imagine the baleful chants of that day when the skies turned red from sadness. I pause on the sidewalk at the spot where you first met Shams, now called the *Merace-Bahreyn*, meaning the "meeting of the seas"; such a paradoxical name for a city located in the middle of dry, dusty plains. I have visited Konya many times, even back when there were no hotels, often bringing groups of women to learn about you and Sufism. When I come to Konya I always expect it to be good, but it is better each time. Everyone is there for one thing:

to receive your love, and I take deep comfort here from being surrounded by people who are searching for the same thing as I am.
How is it that a country and a city could become a soul mate? For
me, Turkey and Konya took on that aspect. I consider myself more
at home there than I do in Paris and I truly feel that I am a *Konevi*
when I am in your city of Konya.

Sometimes I become pensive when I walk the backstreets of
Konya. When I first saw the tomb of Shams, I was startled to see
how dark and foreboding it appeared, not at all radiating blazing light from its walls as I had imagined it would. Echoing along
the alleys of Konya I can hear your sighs of sadness after Shams
left, and I can sense the dread of those difficult days of the mid-
13th century, when all Konya trembled in fear of the approach-
ing Mongols. After they had taken over Anatolia from the Seljuks
in 1243, they razed many cities to the ground, killing thousands
of people in the process. Such a threat did not seem possible at
first for Konya, but in 1256, the Mongols under Commander Baiju
approached the very gates of the city. Legend has it that, miracle
of miracles, they did not enter the city due to your saintly presence there, saving the city and its population from certain dev-
astation. Yet in 1258 the Mongols did capture Baghdad and extin-
guished the ruling house of the Abbasid caliphs, a crushing blow
to Islam. In the same year your pupil and companion, Salah al-din
Zarkub, fell ill and died, and you buried him next to your father.
You had become quite attached to this goldsmith of the spirit,
working together with him for almost ten years. As with Shams,
this friendship was solidified by a marriage, for he gave the hand
of his daughter Fateme to your son Sultan Valad. This illiterate, but
gentle, soul helped you recover from the loss of Shams and to find
yourself again, there in the dust of the goldsmith's bazaar on the
backstreets of Konya. After his death, life continued, and soon a
new chapter opened for you, one none of us could have imagined.

A new chapter opened for me, as well, at this time. Spreading
your word with books, articles, translations, lectures, and appear-
ances on television and radio show was one thing, but I missed
teaching and the vibrant dialogues I had with the young students
at Al-Azhar. However, I realized that I did not need to be in a university in order to teach, but that the salon of my apartment could
become my personal classroom.

It started with one or two young people I would meet at concerts or lectures. Sometimes I would introduce myself; other times, they would come up to me, saying that they were moved by something I said in a public lecture, or by a passage they had read in one of my texts. They would ask me questions that I knew would take longer than just one sentence on the spot to answer. They had such hunger in their eyes and there was such thirst in those questions. So I would give them my telephone number, and tell them to call me for a visit. I did not know how else to answer them on the spot, and soon a steady stream was winding its way up the five flights of stairs of my building on the rue Claude Bernard.

In the Gospel of Matthew, Jesus says: *"Let the little children come unto me and do not hinder them, for to such belongs the Kingdom of Heaven."* You say: *"Do not preach, instead act as a living model. The greatest book to be read is the human being."* The An-Nisa verse of the Qur'an says: *"...do good unto your mother, unto your father, unto orphans and the poor, unto close neighbors and distant neighbors, unto the friend near you, unto the traveler, and unto those who depend upon you."* I now saw that these young travelers depended on me, and I had to be there to help them on their way.

Mevlana, you dispensed your spiritual teaching to many correspondents, friends, and disciples, not just in the medrese, but in small lodges that you founded. Your disciples formed Sufi brotherhoods, called *tariqa*. *"Tariq"* in Arabic means "path, road, way," and it was with these brotherhoods that your message spread. And in a way this is what I am doing as well with these young people. Konya or Paris, what is the difference? A *tariqa* brotherhood can be formed anywhere people will listen to the message of humanity, fraternity, and humility. We are here together on this path, the one you have shown us. Dervishes are expected to treat one another as brothers and sisters – to open their homes, their hearts, and their purses to one another, and so I opened my home to the little children who are, like me, in search of the Absolute.

So many came and so many hours we would spend in communion in the presence of your verses and their meaning! I had so many books in my apartment that I often wondered if we would all fit. We would push aside the stacks of books from the couch and the chairs and put them any place we could find: in the sink, in the bathtub or on the floor, and in the end there was room for all to sit. The conversation flowed as readily as the cups and cups of tea we shared. We were all there in my humble apartment for the same reason: to learn from each other and from you, and many were the evenings when I learned more from them than they did from me. I am certain that all these young people climbing the five flights were looking for something beyond their current existence; beyond what the paving stones thrown during the May '68 demonstrations could give them. In our world there is an increasing imbalance of the spiritual and physical aspects of life. People, especially the young, crave a meaning in life they cannot find in the increasingly consuming society of our times which has so altered religious consciousness. The soaring soul in each of us seeks to take flight, yet our existence is often boxed into a narrow frame. I know your verses are wings for these young people.

The 5th arrondissement of Paris is far from Konya, yet believe me, your sermons and verses resounded in all the languages of my students, coming from all the corners of the world, gathered here in Paris to learn of you, dear Mevlana, a poet from Turkey of the 13th century whose message transcends national and religious boundaries! There was Andrew, an Englishman born in India and filled with more world spiritualties than one could handle. There was Abdullah, my beloved Turkish friend from Konya, sent to me by you, I am certain! He was in Paris to study French literature, and he would accompany me when I would visit his city, taking care of me with the vigilance and tenderness of a son for his mother. He sat by my side, his sweet face smiling at me, like Zarkub must have done with you, Mevlana. Abdullah is the son of my dreams, always present to help me and to support all I do. If I had had a daughter, I would have wanted her to take him as her husband! What a blessed gift bestowed upon me by Allah is that Abdullah! I loved the Belgian Colette; so lovely she was, inside and out, open to learning everything and seeing the world with those clear, blue eyes of hers and her clear, tender heart. There was the lanky Eric who wished to accept Islam and came to me for advice, just as I had done with Massignon so many years before.

Every person is a treasure. For me, there is no spirituality without serving and sharing. To turn to others is to find God, and working with these students has brought me closer to your words which shed such insight. I believe that your teachings and philosophy are the most accessible face that Islam can present to the West. It is difficult for Westerners to apprehend this faith by reading the Qur'an, for it is perhaps too detached from their culture, and I cannot blame them for that. But with your gentle hand showing them the way through your stories and poems, they could see the true beauty of this faith. I wish for people to see that Islam is not about fanaticism and violence, veils, four wives, camels, and tents in the desert; this image pushed into our minds by persistent stereotypes in the press. I hope, too, that Westerners will have more opportunity to discover prominent Islamic thinkers who are so poorly represented in the curriculum of our universities and who have not yet been widely translated into European languages.

Talking with these students has allowed me to put into practice one of the strongest lessons of the Sufi way: service to others. The Sufi way is not a retreat from the world, but a way of seeking the Divine while being actively engaged in the world. You say: *"Keep your hands busy with your duties in this world, and your heart busy with God."* The basic Sufi principle is to pursue high mystical goals, yet, at the same time, to live in the world and participate fully in life. To be a dervish is to love and serve others in pious acts and useful works. Smiling is deed enough, if you are poor! My head cannot be engrossed only in my translations, and it is not enough simply to love: we must *act* upon our love and knowledge, for to serve the created is to serve the Creator. These young people have given me the opportunity to serve.

I must make it possible for people to find an alternative to the wars, conflicts, and materialism of our current world and that is why I devote my life to translating your works and speaking to others about you. It is my hope that people will read the pearls aligned on the pages of your poems, and string them into a luminous necklace they can wear with joy. This is why I rise at dawn to work so hard to crack open the oysters of translation to discover the pearls that will glow for the world and why I talk with young people long into the night. This I do with love for God, for you and for others.

As these young people leave to go back down those five flights and out into the world once again, I repeat to all of them these words of yours: *"Make everything in you an ear, each atom of your being and you will hear in every moment what the source is whispering to you without the need for my words or anyone else's. You are, we all are, the Beloved of the Beloved. And in every moment, in every event of your life, the Beloved is whispering to you exactly what you need to hear and know."*

Chapter 10
The *Sema*: The End of Turning and the Qur'an Reading

The dervish is ready to honor

At the conclusion of the 4th Salutation, the instrumentalists play pieces called the *Last Peshrev* (8-beat measures) and *Last Yürüksemai* (6-beat measures) in an improvisation by a single musician. With this final solo, hearts that were quickened and exuberant in the joy of servanthood are slowly calmed.

The music is interrupted as a *hafiz* from among the singers begins to recite a text of his choosing from the Noble Qur'an. The reading is most often the Bakara verse 2:115: "*Unto God belong the East and West, and whichever direction you turn your face, there is the presence of Allah. He is All-Embracing and All-Knowing.*"

The dervishes immediately stop turning and halt facing the Sheikh. This movement is so quick that their billowing skirts wrap around their legs, like birds swirling down to the trees at sunset. The *semazens* withdraw to the edge of the floor to their places, put their black cloaks back on, and kneel down. They have returned to their tombs, but in an altered state.

The scent of lemons and oranges is in the air; air so dry and pure that your lungs take it in with ease. The sky, filled with delicate wisps of clouds that tickle the low winter light, is as blue as the glittering sapphire waves of the nearby Mediterranean Sea. Bright sun beats down and warms my aged bones and soul. I see mountains in the distance, gleaming in its rays. The abundant sunshine also blesses row upon row of fruit trees; for this is citrus land, where grow the finest clementines in the world.

It is also the land of sweet fruits of another kind, your kind. I am in a remote area of North Africa, in a place where the path of roses now leads me. Clementines and roses; that is what I am living, here, in a white stucco Sufi dervish lodge in Madagh, Morocco.

How did I ever get here from Paris, and how did I find the time to come here in a life that was busier than ever? I continued to hold my post at the CNRS at the same time that I served as director of research at the University of Paris at the Jussieu campus near my home. I was translating deep into the night until dawn, giving lectures, and meeting with the students who climbed the five flights to my home in a steady stream. There were not enough hours in the day for all my work, and yet I knew something was missing. For a long time, I have known that the answers to my lifelong search were not to be found just in books – even those as rich as yours, Mevlana. I knew that it was not just by reading, studying, and translating Sufi masters of the past that I would be able find answers, but that I needed to encounter living representatives of the Sufi tradition. I had already met several of them, such as Amadou Hampaté Ba, Nadjm oud-Dîn Bammate, and the Algerian Khaled Bentounès, and their richness of spirit showed me that I needed to go farther on this quest, even at this advanced age of my life.

I learned from my experience in Cairo and from my other trips abroad that travel is physical as well as metaphysical, actual as well as metaphorical. I knew that travel on the path of roses leads to the ultimate quest of merging with the Divine, but I realized that I still had many miles to go towards that goal. I needed to venture to a place I had never been. I may serve as a teacher to all those young students climbing the stairs to my home, but in truth, it was I who was in need of instruction.

I am curious about everything and every domain, and have been since I was a little girl. Greek philosophy, psychology, English literature, Indian theology, law, knitting, Islamic poetry, everything! I like to ask questions, to find answers and to study hard. I think that old age begins when you lose that curiosity, and I am still inquisitive to learn more and more. This is why I set out to find a living Sufi master who could share his wisdom with me. So, at an age when most women are playing with their grandchildren, I set off to the tip of the land of sweet clementines in northeastern Morocco, an area bounded by the Mediterranean to the north and the Algerian border to the east, far removed from Paris and Konya, yet so close to you.

It is a bit of a miracle that I now find myself in these windswept plains of northeastern Morocco. The hand of one of the students who have been climbing the stairs to my home held out a rose and led me here; a young man whom I now consider as a spiritual son.

Dear, sweet Faouzi! This tender young man was 23 when he came into my life. I remember so clearly when and how we met, as if it were yesterday, for it was no ordinary, chance meeting, but a signpost for both of our destinies.

It was almost ten years ago, back in 1976. I was giving a lecture with the editor Paul Seghers, an orientalist who had recently published a volume of verses by the Persian poet Hafiz. The lecture was held at the FNAC, the legendary Parisian bookstore *cum* cultural center, with its discussion forums, literary fairs and lecture programs. After the lecture, a young man approached me hesitantly and introduced himself. I asked him where he came from, which is the same question I ask everyone I meet, as I am always pleased to see that people from so many different countries are now interested in your work. When he said he came from Fez, I told him that it was my favorite city in Morocco, and then I asked him if he had knew of a certain Moroccan Sufi dervish master named Sidi Hamza. I had recently heard of him and his dervish lodge and I was curious to learn more about him. The young man suddenly started trembling, and I saw that my question had somehow upset him. I quickly grabbed a piece of paper and jotted down my telephone number and told him to call me, for we needed to speak in a place calmer than the bustling crowds of the bookstore. His face was so luminous and gentle that I knew we had to spend more time together, and I felt a bit badly that I had distressed him and wanted to make sure he was alright. Little did I know then that in the upcoming years, he would become one of my most precious friends and intellectual partners.

Two days later Faouzi did call me, and climbed those five flights to my home. During that first visit he related the inconceivable story about our meeting at the FNAC and why he had become so agitated. Inconceivable, yes, but it is a story I believe in, just as I believe that the dream I had about my tombstone was the sign telling me I should embrace Islam. He told me he was heading to his home in the suburbs after a hard day's work as a chimneysweep, and, while waiting for the *métro* to arrive, a strong impulse hit him, so compellingly powerful that he needed to lean against the wall of the subway platform to collect himself. This impulse told him that he needed to go right then and there to the FNAC. He was tired; he wanted to get home to his family, there was soot all over his clothes, and yet this urge would not let go of him. So, despite all logic, he turned around and headed to the FNAC. While wandering through the aisles of this vast palace of knowledge, he wondered why that inner voice had driven him there. He recalled that he had first discovered my translation of your book of sermons, the *Fihi ma Fihi*, on the shelves of this very bookstore and it was perhaps in the hope of finding another book of such powerful inspiration that he had been called there by that voice.

The *Fihi ma Fihi* held much personal significance for him, and, to use the cliché, it was a book that changed the path of his life. He told me that he had, as many young people are wont to do, abandoned his traditions of faith, but while studying at the university in Paris he felt the need to tend to his spiritual development. Just as I had done when I was his age, he meditated and read the sacred texts of diverse religions. Yet, he kept turning to the Sufi texts more and more, and when he read my translation of your *Fihi ma Fihi*, something clicked. He confided to me that it was the inspiration he found in this book that pushed him to question his studies in anthropology and led him to focus on the study of Sufism as it is lived in his native Morocco.

While roaming the aisles of the bookstore that night he hoped to find a similar book, but found nothing, and decided to leave, as this had indeed all been a crazy idea from the start. On the way down the escalator to the exit, he heard a voice over the loudspeakers announcing: *"Eva de Vitray will be giving a talk with the editor Paul Seghers in the auditorium in 15 minutes, come one, come all!"* He froze on the spot and almost stumbled at the bottom of the escalator. He came to my lecture, obviously excited to meet the woman who had opened your verses to him, but above that, he explained to me why my question had agitated him so. After reading your lectures in the *Fihi ma Fihi*, he sought out a Sufi Sheikh to guide him, and this master was none other than the very same person I had asked him if he knew. You can understand now, dear Mevlana, that my meeting with this young man that evening at the FNAC was no mere coincidence, just as it was no coincidence that Shams walked into your life out of the blue.

So began our relationship, which became deep over the years. I encouraged Faouzi to continue with his studies in Sufism and to publish. He took me with him to Morocco on several trips, and it was on one of those voyages that he introduced me to his master. And now here I am, thirty years after becoming a Muslim, following the guidance of a living Sufi master, introduced to me by a young Moroccan man whom I had introduced to Sufism. That irony is worth of one of your fables, Mevlana, and actually brings to mind one of the folktales told by the popular Turkish fabulist Nasreddin Hoja. He was walking along a deserted road in a caravan one night when he spied a troop of horsemen coming towards him. Fearful that they were there to rob him, he ran to hide, leaping over a wall into a cemetery. His fellow travelers became curious and followed him, but not understanding what was going on, one of them asked him: *"Hoja! What in the world are we doing here?"* Nasreddin Hoja responded: *"Well, it is more complicated than you assume. You see, I am here because of you, and you are here because of me."*

Who followed whom in our story? Whom am I following now in my life? Whom did you truly follow, Mevlana? Life can be experienced at many different levels, just as in this fable, and so I suppose, in the end, it is no surprise that I am sitting at the feet of this master, in the windswept hills of Morocco.

You say: *"Man is a book. In him everything is written, but darkness does not allow him to read this science inside himself."* The story of Shams coming into your life and transforming you into an inspired poet had shown me the lesson that you cannot become a Sufi on your own. There is no official instruction manual or textbook on the matter. Of course, it is assumed, just as you encouraged, that a Sufi dervish will adhere to the practices of the five pillars of the Islamic faith – profession of the *shahada*, daily prayer, alms-giving, fasting during the month of Ramadan and pilgrimage to Mecca: that is a given. But beyond that, you need to follow a master; quite literally, you need to go to a "mystical school," run by a Sufi Order (*tariqa*). The *tariqa* meets in a dervish lodge, a building called a *zaviyeh*. Here you study with a teacher, known as a *murshid* or a *sheikh*, along with a group of fellow Sufi students called the *murid*. It is a two-way street: the word *murid* is derived from the word "will" (*irada*), and symbolizes the quest for spiritual achievement, and the master himself must be worthy of being imitated in his understanding of the law, the path and the truth. It is a spiritual agreement which leads two people to share the same interiority, one that the Persian mystics call *ham-dam*, or "being from the same breath."

There are no self-appointed masters in Sufism. In the Sufi Orders, every Sufi teacher has been trained by his own teacher, in an unbroken chain of sheikhs called the *silsila*. The *silsila* starts directly from the teachings of Prophet Muhammad and the other prophets such as Moses and Jesus. Prophets are people who have received a message from God for a whole community, and they pass it to others. The transmission of the spiritual secret, the *sirr,* from the Prophet in this long chain from the master to the disciple is essential, as it comprises a nourishment of the heart that the *murid* would not be able to find on his own. The Prophet Muhammad said: "*The old man (sheikh) among his people is like the prophet in his community.*" The sheikh works though God's spiritual light and serves as a mirror placed in front of the novice to teach him right behavior and to make him acquainted with spiritual truth, reflecting the vision of divine light. In the sheikh, the Hidden Treasure, the 99 attributes of God, are displayed openly for those students who are ready to try to see them.

Mevlana, you know much about being both a student and then a master. Although Shams was not your spiritual master in the ordinary sense, he did play the role of *sheikh* for you in one important aspect: he was the mirror in which you contemplated God's perfection. The role of the sheikh as the full successor of the Prophet is an important concept for you, and a good part of your teachings concerns the nature of the prophets and the saints and the necessity of following them on the spiritual journey. You say: "*Choose a master, for without him this journey is full of tribulations, fears, and dangers. Do not travel alone on the Path,*" and: "*Whoever goes on the path without a guide, for him a way of two days becomes a hundred years.*" In Sufism, the bond between master and disciple is essential. You call him the "*Ladder to*

Heaven," such a touching analogy. You also say one of the most poignant things I have read in the *Masnavi* about this point. You say that the body of each of us is like Mary's, and that we all possess a latent Jesus within us, ready to be born. As a mother, this noble thought of our potentiality moves me deeply.

Thus Professor Hawwa Hanim of Al-Azhar now submitted herself to a master like a young student; yet, somehow, it all seemed natural. I was no longer young, I had traveled around the world, met famous people, published books and spoken to crowds, yet here I was, back sharpening my pencils like the first day of school with the *bonnes soeurs* in Boulogne-sur-Seine. We must always remember that we are nothing but students in this path of life, no matter at what age, and we must always keep alive our potential of growth to climb that ladder, rung by rung.

Finding an authentic voice of Sufism is the keystone of living the Sufi life from the inside out, and, thanks to Faouzi, at the age of 76 I met the living Sufi master who would serve as my spiritual guide. His full name was Sidi Hamza al-Qadiri al-Boutchichi. He became for me, as goes the Sufi expression, *"Not he from whom you hear fancy speeches, but whose presence, his baraka, transforms you."* Sidi Hamza al-Qadiri al-Boutchichi was born in Morocco, and is some ten years younger than I am. Like you, Mevlana, he showed signs of spiritual stature quite early in his life, where his gifts were noted by other Sufis in the area. First at the Madagh *zaviyeh* and then at the University, he learned the traditional sciences of the Hadith, the Qur'an, Islamic jurisprudence, theology, mathematics, rhetoric, and logic, in all of which he excelled and mastered. From there he went on to master the esoteric sciences, and finally became the *silsila* Sheikh of the Sufi lodge at Madagh.

This *zaviyeh* of Sidi Hamza, known as the Tariqa Qadiriyya Boutchichiyya, is similar to many others around the world, including the numerous Mevlevi lodges founded to honor your teachings. *Zaviyeh* literally means "nook," or "corner," and it is the building where the meetings of a Sufi order, or brotherhood of dervishes, are held. Although many *zaviyehs* over the centuries have been simple, one-roomed affairs, this one was a large, modern white building with three floors, including the main lecture space, service areas and lodgings for the dervishes who come here to spend time with the Sheikh. The main assembly room where we generally meet is quite vast, large enough to hold 200 people. Its walls are painted white and have numerous tall windows, and the floor is covered with a sea of identical red prayer carpets. There is no furniture in the room, other than some chests for books and the carpets on the floor. This room is bright, and, as such, reflects the philosophy of Sidi Hamza. He compares a novice's heart with a darkened room in disorder, and to create order, one must first bring in light. He so often says to us: *"Be the guardians of your heart and make it as clean and pure as a prayer space!"* When I sit in this luminous room I think of the light pouring through the enormous stain-glass south rose window of Notre Dame de Paris, and how the same spirit of divine presence fills this simple room as it does the finest cathedral in Europe.

When I first met the Sheikh Sidi Hamza a few years ago, I realized that he was no ordinary personality, yet his physical presence and appearance were unassuming. All benevolence came from his face, round as a juicy Moroccan orange and totally at peace. The Sheikh sat upright on a carpet, cross-legged with his hands on his knees in a hierarchic attitude, yet at the same time, his posture seemed perfectly natural. These days, the Sheikh, now bending to the imperatives of age, rests on a dais propped up by a mountain of thick, white cushions. He wears a tunic and trousers of green silk, the color of the Prophet, and addresses the dervishes who sit before him in rows, dressed all alike in white cotton *djellabas*, the traditional long loose tunic worn in North Africa. We appear before him in the same way that *Hajj* pilgrims in their *ihram* appear before the black Kaaba stone at Mecca. We are all God's children in that room; men and women disciples of diverse age, cultures, ethnicities, nationalities, and professions. I never feel out of place here due to my background, age, or sex. I feel connected to both the Sheikh and the other disciples, and, with each passing day, the bond between us grows stronger and stronger, for we are all here for the same thing: to feel the presence of God and to discover the potential for love within us.

When it was first questioned that I would come here, Sheikh Sidi Hamza requested to meet me privately, I suppose to better ascertain if this elderly European woman was truly serious about joining his *zaviyeh*. When I came in front of the sheikh an astounding experience happened to me, and in many ways, I wonder if it recalls the lightning and magic of your first meeting with your master Shams. He looked at me intently and silently, and then cried out: *"Rumi is here!"* and jabbed the area of his heart with his index finger. His gesture had such an unexpected emotional impact on me that I broke into tears. I knew that this was a sign, like that dream in the cemetery so many years ago, that this *zaviyeh* and its Sheikh were my destiny.

Our days here are comprised of prayer, readings from the Qur'an, sermons, meetings with the Sheikh and guided discussions among the disciples. When Sidi Hamza addresses us his voice is subdued and gentle: there are certainly no thunderous orations from this preacher or fire-and-brimstone admonitions. His manners are courteous and his way of speaking discrete and measured. No word is superfluous. He does not sermonize as much as he opens a new vector of potentiality in us, much like I did with my students at Al-Azhar when I would engage them in Socratic dialogue. Sidi Hamza is able to address each and every one on his own level: man, woman, ordinary Muslim, experienced Sufi, intellectual or illiterate – he reads them all on their own level of spiritual awareness. He often slowly moves his hand in the air when speaking, as if waving his words along to better reach our ears and hearts.

Often, a far-away look takes control of his eyes; other times his gaze bores right at you into the depth of your soul. Sometimes the Sheikh does not speak at all with us, and we sit quietly at his feet. He says that he who understands the value of a Sheikh knows that his relationship with him does not depend on words. You see me and I see you, and that is largely sufficient, he would say.

There are sessions for both men and women, for I am not the only woman who comes here. There had been many women who followed your teachings, Mevlana, for did you not allow women to join your classes at the medrese, to become educated on a par with men? Were not some of your most eager students the young women who flocked to you for that light you could give? There was Sefer Hatun, the daughter of your son Sultan Valad, and who helped to enlighten many female students. There was Arif-i Hoshlika, who founded a *zaviyeh* in the green Seljuk town of Tokat and Gunesh Hatun, who became a sheikh in the *zaviyeh* of Afyon. Despite challenging and changing conditions, these women trained for the *sema* and danced for themselves. And now I dance for you in the circle of your remembrance; here, at the feet of this living Sufi named Sheikh Boutchichi.

Often my lack of perfect Arabic keeps me from understanding completely all that the Sheikh is telling us during his lectures and guidance sermons, and I have to ask the others or my Sufi colleagues once back in Paris for help with the lessons, but I understand the inner meaning, the one that goes deeper than words. Our trusting relationship with the gentle Sidi Hamza is in many ways similar to the relationship between psychotherapist and patient, or even like the emotional connection between mother and child. It is as Sheikh Sidi Hamza says: *"Love is perfect when the love of the disciple towards his sheikh is completed by love of the sheikh for his student."* Yet one thing is certain: I am awakening again to this love and this light, just as the first time I read those lines of yours in the book by Iqbal. I am discovering that same pure love, once again, in a powerful way, and my beliefs are becoming more crystalline and distilled.

Above all, our days are filled with the practice of *dhikr*, an exercise for the divine remembrance of God.

The Qur'an says: *"Remember me and I will remember you."* Dhikr is the systematic repetition of the names and the attributes of God, and honors this line of the Qur'an. *Dhikr* is an essential element of mystical Islam, for it recalls the *tawhid*, the belief in the Unity of God. It also constitutes an *anamnesis* in the Platonic sense. To follow the Sufi path means to remember God constantly, to be aware of Him in every moment, and this is what we learn to do by performing the various spiritual exercises with sincerity of intention, awareness, and concentration. When I first came here, I was given a string of prayer beads, called a *tespih*. Sidi Hamza taught me to recite words using the *tespih* to count them out. He explained that in doing this I would begin my journey down a path towards filling my heart with the presence of God.

Dhikr is a beautiful practice. It begins with the repetitive affirmation of the formula "There is no god but God." At the outset, the repetition of *La ilaha illallah* becomes the junction point between heaven and earth. This repetition is the remembrance of the tongue. Later, the repetition creates a temporary, inner state in which awareness of God overwhelms you and you become truly divorced from all concerns for the world, at least for the moment you are repeating the phrase. This is the remembrance of the heart. Finally, it leads to a deep and stable inner station in which invocation and mindfulness become constant. This is the remembrance of the soul.

Sidi Hamza is a firm believer in the potential of *dhikr*. He says, *"Try to keep your interior clean and pure, and dhikr will help you rid from that which is impure inside of you. Every person is a slave to something, except those who are free inside of themselves. Do lots of dhikr and you will become free as well!*" Here at the *zaviyeh* we practice *dhikr* in many ways. Sometimes we chant one of the 99 names of Allah – "patience" was my favorite one to repeat. In the same fashion we listen to songs called *qasida*, which are a sort of Islamic hymns, played back on a tape player or performed by live musicians. The emotional voice of Sidi Hamza often joins the incantations, and these sessions often bring tears to my eyes. Other times we perform a group recital of *dhikr* called the *wadifa*, filling each person with the light of God in a manner more inclusive than when the *dhikr* is made alone.

Sometimes the novice dervishes remain motionless and silent for hours at a time. Other days, the dervishes sit in circular groups and softly start a lingering chant, and sway from side to side as they repeat the name *"Allah"* with each movement, sometimes fast, sometimes slowly, depending on how their spirit moves them. Some dervishes become breathless, others burst into tears, and once in a while a dervish sobs or cries out with a long, drawn out *"Allah!"* Others fall to the ground in exhaustion in a state of *hal,* or spiritual ecstasy, an intense moment when your soul recognizes the presence of God.

As psychologically perturbing as these outbursts appeared to a Cartesian person such as myself, they did not frighten me in the least. I have studied enough psychology to know the restless states of agitation that are possible for the psyche. To a normal outsider and for the rational mind, such uncontrolled outbursts like this seem implausible, and even spurious and ludicrous, and yet, believe me, the state of *hal* is very, very real. The lines from Psalm 130 come to my mind: *"Out of the depths have I cried unto Thee, O Lord."* All who come here are crying out to the Lord and the Sheikh is here to guide those supplications. All come to the *zaviyeh* to seek inward peace and self-realization in God, and all find it in the way they can, and more or less to their capacities, rising higher towards that goal than when they first came. These extemporaneous outbursts show me that the path to experience the presence of God can take many forms, from a quiet and deeper warmth, to being out of control in ecstatic excitement.

When I first came here, I would hold those *tespih* beads in my hand and would repeat the words taught to me by the Sheikh over and over again, and not much time passed before the power of these words had their effect. I began to feel intense feelings of the presence of God that were similar to the many decisive prophetic dreams that I had experienced in the past. I now more than ever understood that dreams, which have been such a part of my life, are a glimpse at the world of the unseen and a subconscious form of *dhikr*. I believe I have found in the practice of *dhikr* the key to all the investigations that have been inside of me since I was that little girl questioning the *bonnes sœurs*: one must repeat the essential in order to remember the essential, and when that memory becomes permanent, the door to the Divine presence opens wide.

You know all about the practice of *dhikr*, Mevlana, for you created what is perhaps the most well-known form of *dhikr* known in the Sufi tradition: the *sema*, the whirling you used to express your love for God, where dervishes rotate in a circle like the vertiginous spinning of the planets around the sun, repeating the word "Allah" with each turning footfall.

You say: *"Many roads lead to God and I have chosen the way of dance and music."* After Shams left you bereft, you worked with Salah al-din Zarkub, the goldsmith, who helped you recover from the loss of Shams. Legend has it that the sound of his tapping hammer in the goldsmith's bazaar in Konya inspired you to turn in mystical rapture in the middle of the street and a new form of expression for the Beloved was born in you.

You found yourself again, there in the dust of the goldsmith's bazaar, and created a ceremony for the wonder and remembrance of God that is unique in the world. Contrary to what many Westerners believe, the *sema* is a not an irregular ecstatic movement done by a group of dervishes who have lost control of themselves, but rather, a harmonious art in which every step is prescribed according to a fixed ritual. The *sema* ceremony flows as beautifully as the words from your pen. Although it was you who inspired the whirling, it was your son, Sultan Valad, who organized the Mevlevi brotherhood and codified the *sema* ceremony we know today.

In between my periodic trips here to Morocco, I continue to write in Paris and travel, especially to Turkey. Between the ages of 78 and 80, I published five books, some of which are translations and others original works about you, Sufism, and Islam. The one book that gave me much joy to write was a book on the city of Konya, my second home, which I wrote in order to relate its history to better draw the reader into your world. It was also a bit of a thank-you letter to your city in appreciation for the honorary doctorate which the Selçuk University awarded me in 1978 for the services I had done to promote your work. At that time they also made me an honorary citizen of the city, and I was so proud to share that happy moment with my adopted Konya son, Abdullah, at my side. I also continue to translate Iqbal, for I have never abandoned my intellectual fascination for him. Yet, when I raise my head from my work desk and look out the window at the grey skies of Paris, I find that my heart keeps returning to the bright and sunny days of peace in Morocco.

One of my favorite moments of the year is in January when the piles of the bright orange jewels of clementines crown the fresh produce displays at the food market of the rue Mouffetard next to my home. Each time I peel a clementine and its tangy aroma hits my nostrils, I am reminded of my time in Morocco.

I peel a slice for me, a slice for you, a slice for Sidi Hamza, a slice for my fellow dervishes, a slice for my students, a slice for peace, a slice for fraternity, a slice for love, a slice for all those in the world who need to understand that we are all segments of the same delicious fruit of life.

Although I am always sad to leave Morocco and Sidi Hamza and my fellow dervishes with whom I have established a strong bond of love, I know that my true duty is to bring back that love and incorporate it into my daily life in Paris. I leave Morocco and return to Paris each time with a deeper understanding of how I can be on the Sufi path, even in the middle of this sophisticated European capital, with all its glamour and distractions. I now know that living the Sufi life means to love and to be of service to people, to desert your ego, to worship God, and to strive to be as perfect as you can be in the eyes of God. Sufism for me represents a mental harbor from our consumer society. It teaches us to privilege personal development and encompassing respect in our relations with others and to always remember the blessings of life. It offers hope to confront the barbarity of a world increasingly harsh. It is a love poem to the finest destiny we can be. I have learned all these things first from you and then at the feet of Sidi Hamza, and I will keep returning here for more and more insight until the end of my days, for what you, Mevlana, and he have given me is the glorious privilege to practice this faith in its purest form.

Chapter 11
The *Sema*: The *Niyaz* Dedication and Farewell Prayers

The dervish is ready to pray

After the reading of the Holy Qur'an is finished, the Sheikh recites the *Fatiha*, the first chapter of the Qur'an, and then kisses his red pelt, the symbol of the divine presence. Sometimes a special prayer in Persian, called the *Gülbanki*, is read by the *semazenbashi*. This long prayer is recited for Mevlana and all the holy men of the Mevlevi order who are mentioned by name, as well as for the salvation of the souls of the prophets, for the people who have died on the path of Allah and for all believers.

After the prayer is finished, the Sheikh and the musicians rise and all the dervishes kiss the floor and rise. The Sheikh leads an invocation to begin vocalizing the sound of "Hu," the divine pronoun encompassing all the names of God. All the musicians and dervishes join in sounding the "Hu" in one voice, until no breath is left in their lungs.

You say: *"I have not sent the Masnavi for you to hold it or to repeat it, but to put it under your feet so that you can fly."*

For the past 15 years I have been flying with you, and now I can put your words under the feet of others. Today, this bird folds her wings and puts her pen down on her desk. I have at last finished the translation of your final and major work, this masterpiece of the literary heritage of humanity known as the *Masnavi*.

The life of a Mevlevi Sufi is based on *adab*, discipline, and *erkan*, rules of conduct. Like a novice dervish in a *zaviyeh*, I certainly studied hard and followed discipline. I worked five hours a day for 15 years on this translation! I prayed to God each day that I would be given enough years to finish it. Yet it was done for love, for God, for you and, I pray, for the people I hope will one day read these verses, for I know that the Occident thirsts for this spirituality.

Over these past 15 years there were times I thought I was insane to do this; totally insane; for who else but a madwoman would care to devote hour upon hour every day, month in and month out, year after year, to translate 51,000 lines of Persian poetry? Insane, yes, but possessed of the quest for beauty. Possessed, just as you were when you first wrote these verses. I know my true function in life is submission and servitude to God, and what better way was there to do this than by translating this massive text? Yet, what an opus you left me to tackle; a gigantic and indefinable work in a class by itself! It is full of admirable legends and lessons and passages of intuition as bright as lightning. I could never decide whether it was a book of poetry, a philosophical system, a general commentary on Islamic theology, an exposé of mystical thought, a metaphysical doctrine, a case study of human psychology, an insightful exposé of the ethnographical and social mores of the daily life of your era, or an educational manual for the techniques of teaching through parable. It is all these things and more. But whatever you intended it to be, of one thing I am certain: you wanted to pack beauty into each couplet, and that, you certainly did. For 15 years, your light was the ink in my pen, and it never ran dry.

Your *Masnavi*! Only the Bible can compare in breadth to this gigantic and indefinable work, this *"jug that contains the ocean"* as you say in the twentieth verse. Its full name is the *"Masnav-i*

Ma'navi" which means "Rhyming Couplets of Deep Spiritual Meaning." The word "Masnavi" means the literary form of rhyming couplets which were used in the work. Your work is full of these couplets: 25,618 to be exact, comprised of two rhyming phrases of eleven syllables each, filling six books in all, each one with some 4,000 verses and its own prologue.

I was astounded at what you had to say in these verses! Each of the six books contains about a dozen major stories and many shorter ones. You took traditional folktales, your own thoughts and musings, events of the day, anecdotes, philosophic discourse, invented stories and prayers and wove them all together into a thick carpet of didactic poetry. You took inspiration for the out-pouring of these verses from many sources: the *Masnavis* written by other Sufi poets, such as Sanai and Attar, the *Shahname*, the book of the legendary exploits of the Persian kings before the Islamic era, the popular Persian love stories of Ferhad and the tragic *Leyla and Mejnun*, as well as the writings of well-known Arab poets. You found much to imitate in the animal fables of the 4th century San-skrit book of *Kalilah wa Dimna* – oh, I loved how you used animals to reveal insights more perceptively than humans could! Yet, in truth, your deepest inspiration in this majestic flowing river of six books is the Qur'an, for almost one quarter of the *Masnavi* consists of direct translations or paraphrases of the Qur'an. You drew heavily as well upon the sayings of the Prophet Muhammad and the stories of the prophets and saints. You, a devout Muslim, obviously wanted the *Masnavi* to be an indirect commentary on the Qur'an and the nature of spirituality in the Islamic religion, capable of carving a path that can lead people toward the Divine presence of a loving God, the primary source to achieving the potential within the human soul. The Qur'an is the beacon you use to light the path, and your stories and mystic thoughts are the stepping stones along this exploration of the inner self.

In fact, all through the *Masnavi*, your mission was to focus on general questions of belief, behavior, and mystical issues to show us that spirituality is universal. Love for God cannot be contained in a label such as Muslim, Christian, and Jew, for when there is complete submission to God, labels fall away and the sincerity of each individual becomes his true worth. You considered doctrine secondary to the goal of touching the heart of your listener and helping him to praise God and to evolve, in the most possible way, into a Perfect Man – that is, to become the best example of what a Muslim can be.

But what a boggling puzzle you put in front of me! When I first began to investigate your work, I was more perplexed by its disjointed structure than I was by understanding the archaic Persian language of the text. For a Cartesian-trained, rational scholar such as myself, this lack of organized form and content was at first quite disconcerting. In French literature we are rigidly exacting in the structure of our compositions, which are based on the Hegelian triad of a thesis, antithesis, and synthesis. We have a beginning, a middle, and a conclusion, neatly wrapped up in a ribbon. Your writings and thoughts, on the other hand, are disjointed and in no discernable order. This chaos often made it difficult for me to synthesize your message, and this was baffling – that was until I understood what you were trying to achieve in your decision to be haphazard in your writing. This was not a trick you were playing on us; no, you knew exactly what you wanted the reader to discover as he wound his way through your stories, discursive anecdotes and verse: his own path – the Sufi path. That path often has detours and challenges, just like the structure of your books. You knew, as well, that peppering your writing with themes sprouting in every direction would continually grab the attention of the reader. Your apparently unstructured presentation is an example of the "scatter" method of teaching favored by Sufis – and, in many ways, it is like the Socratic method I used with my students by asking them a simple question, formulating objections, refining the answers, and pulling in other connections. As a teacher, you knew that each student is different and that you had to reiterate a key point – such as the fall of man through pride – in several different fashions throughout the six books to make sure that, in the end, its message could be understood by all stations of men, from the peasant to the learned.

Your verses are human and spiritual at the same time. The whole *Masnavi* is an attempt to illustrate the Qur'anic verse: *"Everywhere you turn is the face of God"* and you were able to see symbols of God in every tiny detail of life. You say: *"Everything is a sign for those who know how to see."* The outward form of the world and everything within it manifests a hidden meaning. You saw the signs which God has put into the world – in the stars, the moon, trees, and even the humble chickpea – and you interpreted them in your stories to show that there is a permanence subsisting beyond the ephemera of our daily lives. These marvelous tales transmit a moral or a mystical truth in an accessible, concrete way, calling into play the imagination and allowing the reader to easily remember them. The stories symbolically depict a voyage of the soul into itself. In reading them, man, asleep in his unconscious daily existence of the ego, will awaken his hidden potential and find himself on the path to God. Your stories, through both their humor and realism, take the reader like a gentle hand guiding him to discover the path, to understand a lesson and to build a bridge of deeper understanding of the divine. You say: *"The book of the Sufi is not written with ink and letters; it is only a heart, white like snow."*

"Words are veils, trees are pens and the ocean is ink," you say. Yes, in this book you were able to condense the entire world into a few lines of poetry and to translate the most complex of spiritual questions into a plain metaphor or a homespun story. How were you able to do that, Mevlana? To explain the deepest truth of life in simple stories is not an easy thing to do. That was the rare genius of Jesus, and you shared that gift with him. You tell enthralling stories with all kinds of subjects, in both lofty language and language of the marketplace. Your voices are fresh and lively and the tone changes so often that no one ever gets bored. Your images and inspirations come from the world around us: cracked water pots, blood, spring flowers, onions, the full moon, roast meat, sweet breezes, ugly women, deer and dogs, old shoes, the weaving loom, and the kitchen; everything on earth is a way for you to explain that love is calling us to the Beloved God and that all is a higher reality. You speak of animals and merchants and Mary and the Resurrection in one breath and all with equal ease. You tell ribald stories with innuendos and brazen images that make me blush, such as the story of the servant girl and the well-endowed donkey. You are capable of dark stories that make me shudder in horror. I roared with laughter at your hilarious stories depicting the follies of stupid merchants and country bumpkins. How could I have ever gotten bored translating all of this? And I never did, for your constantly whirling world of images kept me challenged, entertained, and inspired for more than 15 years. *"Forty camels would not be able to carry my book if I were to tell everything on my mind,"* you say, and I believe that this is true. I never wanted to put my pen down and sleep lest one of your images flee my mind. I have not

regretted one minute of the time and energy that it took me to translate your *Masnavi*: my exhaustion, my denial of pleasures and relaxation and the estrangement from my sons; no, I sacrificed all for you, so that these magnificent verses could be opened to others. Such is my love for you; such is the gift of my white heart in black ink to you.

"Love has a hundred tongues!" you say. Trying to put those hundreds of tongues into the one French language was a challenge that defied the seven valleys of my life. I was no inexperienced writer when I began this project, for I had already translated and written 30 books. Yet the challenge of this colossal translation was not just one of hours and hours of eyes strained, gallons of midnight oil burned, sleep lost and meals missed. Nor was the size of the *Masnavi* the most daunting trial in front of me, and long it certainly was. Alas, you could not save me, dear Mevlana, from the fundamental paradox that faces every translator. If a translation is to be faithful, it must also be in some ways inevitably unintelligible, for all cannot be translated. Such is the secret magic inherent to every original language.

It was such a test to translate this book! How was I able to combine the precision of your words with the notes I felt I needed to add to make them understandable to Western readers? How could I attempt to convey the inner from the outer meaning, to give the literal sense of the words you wrote without explaining either their metaphorical or mystical sense? Ah, but this is the Sufi paradox, the seen and the unseen; for we know that all on this earth, including your words, are nothing but signs and signifiers of the Divine. Yet some of your passages just remained so mysterious, and I felt I did not possess the key to open the door to them. I would scratch my head wondering to whom you were speaking: was it to your circle of intimate friends or your disciples or the very Sultan himself? Were you speaking with your own voice or with the voice of one of the animals you so loved to use to expound your philosophy? How I would get lost as you slid from narrative into discourse and your descriptions and addressees changed like flowing water! For all this and more, on countless nights I would pray for guidance, and I was so fortunate to have the aid of Djamchid Mortazavi to clarify many of my questions. The final challenge I faced was to render it all gracefully into the subtleties of the magnificent

French language – a language so delicate and precise that no sloppiness can be tolerated.

My dear mentor Louis Massignon, an accomplished translator of the Arabic language, used to say to me that the words of the poet are an invitation for the translator to go beyond language and to give an even purer sense to the words. He spoke of the necessity to leave behind your mother tongue and original culture to better perceive the deep meanings that spring forth in the alchemy of language and music that constitutes poetry. He was right. The transposition of your words into my maternal language allowed me to measure the impact of your thought. It wasn't just a question of recognizing and translating words, but of understanding the deep and subtle meanings as well as the flavor of everything behind them. To be a translator is not just a job, it means living in communion with another civilization.

I was not just a translator of your text: I lived with your text inside of me like an unborn child. I fell asleep at night with your verses in my head, they woke me at dawn and they filled my thoughts all day long. Sometimes I would speak to you as if you were sitting next to me at my work table, asking you for advice on a thought or a phrase. I would set out on my day with your words in my head, and I would try to live them in my encounters with others and with my intellectual enquiries. You were my constant companion. I worked closely with you all these years, just as you originally worked on text with Husamuddin Chelebi, your favored and faithful pupil, for some ten years.

After the burning love with Shams and the spiritual peace you found with Zarkub, you were able once again to find inspiration for a third time in the person of Husamuddin Chelebi. You became Husamuddin's teacher, guide, and master, and he repaid you with one of the dearest gifts of all: motivation and encouragement. As you entered the twilight of your years, you decided to spend more time in meditation, prayer, and writing. You appointed Husamuddin, who came from the merchant class, to run the financial affairs of your school, and then you retired from active involvement in the affairs of the world. Yet Husamuddin would not let you withdraw from life, for he felt there was still so much for you to do. It was he who prodded you to commit to paper your thoughts, ideas, and teaching themes for the benefit of your disciples. He did not want you to leave this world without a written trace, as Socrates had done!

As the story goes, one day around the year 1262, when you were about 55 years old, Husamuddin Chelebi approached you and told you how he wished that you could produce a work in verse in the style of Attar's *Conference of the Birds*. You apparently immediately pulled out a piece of paper tucked inside your turban on which were written the first 18 lines of the *Masnavi*, and said to him, *"I will speak these if you will write them down."* And in this way started the joint project of the dictation and recording of the *Masnavi*.

For the next several years, Husamuddin followed you like a shadow down the back streets of Konya wherever you went, writing down every verse that flowed from your lips. He would quickly write as you composed, singing back what he had recorded for your confirmation and approval. He would correct it, add words and tenses and edit it. Sometimes you spoke so quickly that he could not catch all the words or understand all your jumping thoughts, but he never gave up. Poor Husamuddin became completely bereft when his dear wife passed away, and went into mourning, but after a while he returned and continued to write your thoughts down until your very last illness.

And now, in this year 1990, I am finished with this gigantic translation, and I am totally spent: I have worked so hard on this text! I am 81 years old now, and each grey hair on my head and each ache in my back are dedicated to one of your couplets, Master Mevlana, and I endured them gladly. I do not know how many years I have left to live, yet I can die happy, for I have made a magical and precious dream come true.

Yet I did not go to all this work, 15 years of hard work, for this translation to sit on my desk. It had to take flight. Now that I had finished my translation, an even more daunting challenge faced me: getting it published. What editor would take on the commercial risk to publish a book this large by an unknown Islamic poet of the 13th century, a book that would probably run to a thousand or so pages, an editor's nightmare? Some ten years ago I had written a preface to a book that had been published by an independent editor in Monaco, les Editions du Rocher, and I knew they had a reputation for taking on daring projects. I made an appointment with their editor, the dignified Monsieur Jean-Paul Bertrand, and on the appointed day, I dressed in my finest suit and sat down in front of him and, using all my powers of persuasion, boldly told him that I had a substantial project for him to consider. He listened to me and slowly nodded, and at the end of the interview, he agreed to take on the project. What daring for him to gamble on publishing a book in six hefty volumes of over 1,100 pages! But courageously he took on this project, and Les Editions du Rocher became a publishing legend in the process.

You will forgive me, Mevlana, for one small trespass: I changed your title, because I wanted people to better understand the depth of your *Masnavi*. I felt that the word "Masnavi" seemed too distant and foreign a word to speak to the Western reader, so I changed it to *The Quest of the Absolute*. I did not want anything to get in the way from people picking up this book, reading it and flying with it!

Perhaps the biggest joy for me is that now that I have finished this translation, I can step back and stop looking at this text under the magnifying glass of the translator, and contemplate it as a reader and a seeker. An entirely different experience now awaits me with your words; this time as a disciple.

Your *Masnavi*, at the time of its writing, was considered to be of such sublime quality in its insights and literary techniques that it achieved instantaneous fame among the educated circles of the day. Your verses have influenced Muslim thought and culture ever since. I wonder how my translation will be received: will people like it? But more than that, will they read it? It seems more than ever, that it *must* be read, for its message must touch more and more people. At this moment in 1990, Operation Desert Shield is unfolding in the Persian Gulf region, in response to Iraq's invasion of Kuwait and the brutality of Saddam Hussein. When will all the senseless violence end?

You say: *"Your soul each moment struggles hard with death; think of your faith as though it's your last breath. Your life is like a purse, and night and day are counters of gold coins you've put away."* Each one of the 26,000 verses of your *Masnavi* is a glistening gold coin in the purse of my soul. I consider myself the richest woman alive, thanks to you, Mevlana. Such a journey we have accomplished together, you and I!

Chapter 12
The *Sema*: Departure of the *Postnishin* and Closure

The dervish is ready to love

After the final "Hu" is pronounced, the Sheikh takes a few steps forward and salutes the *semazenbashi*, who returns the greeting. During this salutation, both of them hold their voices in the same tone and extend the salutation for a few seconds. After this, the Sheikh takes a few more steps and repeats the process with the *neyzenbashi*.

The Sheikh bows to the red sheepskin *post* and crosses the floor and walks out of the hall. The *semazenbashi* movement master, musicians, and dervishes calmly file out of the *semahane*, each bowing toward the red sheepskin as they cross the center line of the floor. All leave the Hall of Celestial Sounds in tranquility, humility, and silence, their hearts having been moved in enraptured flight and ecstasy in the cosmic dance of harmony. They are ready to return to the world with love in their hearts.

It is summer and it is very warm. The sunlight pours through the open windows of my 5th floor apartment, reflecting off the parquet floor in blinding patches. As I lie here in my bed, this bed from which I can no longer rise, I think of the path we have traveled together in this *sema* of our lives, separated by over 700 years, yet as close together as two petals on a rose. You died, Mevlana, soon after the completion of the *Masnavi*. How much time do I have left on this earth? I am 90 years old now, but I am not yet ready to put down my pen. Whatever energy is still left in me is at your service, for each one of your verses is a second heartbeat to me; in this heart of mine which seems to be beating slower with each passing day.

How quickly these past few years since the completion of my translation of your *Masnavi* have flown by! Even though the biggest translation challenge of my life was over, my pen was busier than ever. The same year that the *Masnavi* was published, I also completed a translation of your *Letters*, the first time they had been rendered in a European language. I spent many hours as well each day answering the correspondence I received from people all over the world, asking me about my books, to discuss a point in one of my lectures, or to ask questions about you.

I continued to work as the co-director of a research group on Islamic cultures for the University of Paris VII as long as I was physically able to do so. I pursued more translation projects, including one on the work of the Sufi poet Shabestari, which had the evocative title: *The Secret Rose Garden*, as well as more translations of your poems. I was also interviewed by an earnest journalist couple. In our frank dialogue, I shared my most sincere thoughts on Islam, the message of love in your teaching, the meaning of Sufi fables, the importance of humility and the quest for fraternity. I wanted to reveal the other face of Islam, the face increasingly obliterated by fundamentalism and power struggles, so that its message can be heard by as many as possible.

I also spent much time with Faouzi, the young Moroccan I met at the FNAC who introduced me to Sidi Hamza. We always had such wonderful discussions about religion in general, and I was always eager to talk to him about the place of Jesus in the Sufi tradition, since it links my past and present lives in harmony. I discovered that he was as interested in learning as much about Jesus from me as I was interested in learning about the Prophet Muhammad from him. We decided to write up our conversations in the form of a modest book entitled *Jesus in the Sufi Tradition* and it became one of my most cherished books. I assembled as many different oral and written Islamic stories, anecdotes, and sources as I could that spoke of Jesus and how he was regarded in the Islamic faith. I wanted to write a book in simple, clear, and expressive French, without any ideological, pedagogical, or confrontational tones in it. I wanted my examples to speak for themselves; to show the privileged place that Jesus and Mary held in the Qur'an and in Islamic thought – for is not Mary, *"the Garden of Spring,"* the only woman mentioned by name in the Qur'an? Is not Jesus referred to in the Qur'an as a prophet in service to God, and is it not he, *"of the sweet smile"* you cited so often in your verses, Mevlana? Did you not say that everyone has a potential Jesus within him? Writing this book gave me the possibility to use the example of Jesus to unite the richness of the Eastern and Western religious traditions with sensitivity and respect. I also discovered a new dimension to my understanding of the message of Jesus, far deeper than what I learned from the *bonnes soeurs*.

I believe that if you had to find a Christian analogy to the Prophet Muhammad, he should be compared to Mary and not to Jesus. Muhammad could not read or write, and thus was a virgin to all knowledge and learning. The revelation of the Qur'an to him was like the virgin birth of Jesus by Mary: the presence of God made manifest. I would also compare the Qur'an itself to the human person of Jesus. Both were methods in which to transmit the message of God: Jesus by his human existence and teachings, and the Qur'an by the written word.

Perhaps you appealed to me so strongly, Mevlana, because you resemble Jesus in so many ways. Like Jesus, you are suspicious of all forms of wealth and power. Like Jesus when he drove the money changers from the Temple, you can be ferocious with your words. Like Jesus, you know that spiritual transformation is not an easy one, and that the path is filled with sharp stones and crowns of thorns. Like Jesus, you are humble, and you know that the path is one we can never finish, for it is as boundless as love itself. Like Jesus, you know the price that one must pay for such dedication.

You both spent time in deserts of despair and Rose Gardens of rapture. Above all, the teaching parables of Jesus are similar to the esoteric language you used in your fables. Both Jesus and the Sufis teach the same lessons: to renew the interior dimension, to suppress the ego, to let love and consideration for others grow, to invite the heart into life and to go beyond religious barriers into a true dialog with God. I saw that the relation that Jesus shared with his disciples was the same as what Mohammed lived with his companions and the Sufi masters foster with their students. So many links exist between our two traditions, lest we not forget it!

Yet, if truth be told, over the past five years I have not been feeling well, and I found my thoughts turning more and more to the subject of prayer. Iqbal had much to say about prayer, and he has helped me to understand the differences in prayer between the Islamic and Christian faiths: for the former it is communal expression of recognition; for the second, an individual dialogue with God. Iqbal said that the posture of the body during prayer was a determining factor for the attitude of the spirit. By that I believe that he meant that a unified direction for Islamic prayer assured a unified sentiment of social equality among all participants. It is certain that when you stand shoulder to shoulder in one line reciting in unison the *Fatiha* chapter in prayer there is no superiority of rank or race. This notion of equality in prayer is capital in Islam, for it demonstrates the essential unity of mankind, and breaks down barriers between humans.

When Muslims hear the *ezan*, the call to prayer, they go to a place where they can pray together as a community. For a Muslim, the collective prayer in a mosque is the best possible form of prayer, and anyone who has gone to Mecca can attest to the profound impact of this humanity of prayer. Yet, collective prayer is not only communal, but it is also individual, for it reinforces the uniqueness of each person. Each person praying does not melt into the community, but rather draws energy from the strength of the community to reinforce his own individuality. The individual is at the heart of Islam, and although the concept of the entire nation of believers, the *umma*, is essential, it must be remembered that the initial step towards this faith, the pronouncing of the *shahada*, is always done alone.

I have also understood that the *Fatiha* chapter, the only prayer recited standing up and which is repeated by Muslims in every prayer series, 40 times per day, is much like the *Pater Noster* prayer I recited in my youth.

Yet prayer is not done just in the mosque. God is everywhere and so can be the recognition of Him. The presence of God can manifest itself at any given moment, without calling, be it in felicitous meetings, in moments of intellectual lucidity, a bright bird flying in the air, or in an everyday event. Mevlana, you spoke of the intimate conversations between man and God – a God who longs to be known, loved, and worshipped and therefore creates the world and all that is in it. Above all, you taught me that prayer is a permanent opening of the heart to God, to others and the universe as a whole, at every second of the day and with every heartbeat.

I decided to capture all these reflections in a book on prayer in Islam. It took many prayers for me to finish this book: there were days I was so tired that I could not pick up my pen but rather had to dictate my thoughts to be written down by my young assistant, just as you did with Husamuddin Chelebi. This will be perhaps my last book – and for certain, my last prayer will be for you.

Lying in my bed these past few months has given me much time to reflect on my life and the reality beyond understanding of the path I have taken. My life and yours have been wound together as tightly as the curls of wool on the red sheepskin of the *postnishin*. We have been two blooming red rose buds on the same branch in the garden of life and together we have been on a long, whirling way towards a truth that both of us desperately sought with every turn of our lives. I have no regrets for anything I have done, despite all the difficulties I encountered. My most cherished job was being a teacher, to make known what I believe to be the true face of Islam, the one of universalism. I have worked hard to dissipate misunderstandings and prejudices against the Islamic faith. I have tried to show that the Sufi tradition has its perfect place in the heart of Islam; that it is not a marginal school or a folkloric tradition, but rather one that harbors all the treasures of wisdom in a message that can be understood by all peoples of all eras on all continents in the world. The word "Islam" means "submission" and I must admit I feel that this word lends itself to much confusion, because it implies the abnegation of the human free will. I prefer to translate it in another way. For me, to be a Muslim means to deliver yourself in peace to God. This deliverance, or this total abandon of the self to the will of God, is the communal core of every religion in the world.

To move beyond separation and fear, we need to appreciate our core teachings and share them. I have learned much from the practices of others: the Protestantism of my grandmother, the Catholicism of my schooling, the Judaism of my husband, the atheism of colleagues and now Islam. I have seen how they all interweave with each other to help us live a more meaningful existence. I have understood that Judaism stands for oneness, a single heavenly being and that we are all part of this one God and that we are all interconnected. From Christianity I have learned the principle of unconditional love and forgiveness, and the beautiful words of Jesus never leave my head: *"But I say to you, love your enemies and pray for those who persecute you. This is my commandment: that you love one another as I have loved you."* From Islam, I have learned compassion. All but one of the 114 chapters of the Qur'an begins with *"Bismillah ir-Rahman ir-Rahim, in the name of God, the merciful."* Compassion is the essence of God and defines God's message to humanity and Islam has taught me that our journey of life should be filled with compassion for the self and others. All these varied spiritual practices – yet so unified in their messages – help us awaken to the greater self – the one beyond our little separate selves – into the big world of humanity. Sufism has taught me that the major religions and mystical traditions of the world share the same essential Truth. There is one message told by many prophets, all illuminating humanity with their light. Spirituality goes beyond the divide between those who believe and the atheists. It goes beyond the codes of one set religion. The finest faith is the one that makes you the best that you can be. It is the faith that allows you to go to the farthest reaches of your soul, and, in doing so, to discover the truth of all the other faiths. It is to go to the center of the circle of acceptance and deliverance unto God and to live a life filled with goodness, generosity, humility, and honesty. This is what the faith of Islam has allowed me to do.

Your life as well showed me that such deliverance is possible. What a full life you led, Mevlana! Then, one day, after a life of writing more than 30,000 verses of lyrical poetry, the 26,000 verses of the *Masnavi*, your letters, your sermons as noted down by your students, you became tired and put down your pen. You fell ill in the winter of 1273. Doctors of every religion attended you, unable to diagnose your ailment. You accepted the inevitable with grace.

Among your parting words to your students, you said, *"I have two things I am attached to in this world; one of them is this body and the other is all of you. When, by God's mercy, I am removed from the world of loneliness and distraction, my attachment to you will yet remain."* How I can understand those words, for am forever indebted to my students for all the love and insight they have given me!

You passed away on December 17, 1273, a night forever more to be known as the *Şeb-i Arus,* or the Night of Union. When you were laid to rest, men of five faiths followed your bier. All the citizens of Konya, adult and child alike: men, women, children, common folk and nobles, Christians, Jews, Greeks, Arabs, and Turks, all came out to watch you pass by, weeping and sobbing and tearing at their breasts. Leaders from all the religious communities joined in the procession, reading from the Psalms, the Torah and the Gospels. The Christians said, *"He is our Jesus."* The Jews said, *"He is our Moses."* The Muslims said of you, *"He is the light and secret of the Prophet. He is the endless sea of goodness."* The memorial *sema* and music went on for hours. Your pet cat refused to eat and died after one week and was buried near you. All Konya cried until there were no tears left, and then its streets fell silent. But not for long. Soon a tomb, the Green Dome, was built over your grave; there in the sultan's rose garden, and ever since the first day it first opened its doors, the dust of the feet of pilgrims making their way there raises a cloud over Konya that can be seen for miles distant.

Before you died, you sent the Sufi poet Fahreddin Iraki to Tokat to set up a dervish lodge in this famous Seljuk city. You encouraged your female students to learn and reach for the same spiritual awareness as men. After your death, your son Sultan Valad took over your teaching responsibilities and began to seriously promote the Sufi movement. He unified the disciples, set up lodges in many cities, and codified the *sema* ceremony. Now there are dervishes throughout the world, from Turkey to Morocco to America.

Mevlana, you lived a life of refinement and scholarship in Konya, much as I have, here in my beautiful world of Paris. You met with the higher strata of society, even daring to upbraid the mighty Seljuk Sultan Alaeddin Keykubad on his behavior. You counseled lofty politicians and ministers like the Grand Viziers Karatay, Muineddin Süleyman and Sahip Ata, and yet you paid the most attention to the little people, the artisans and merchants: weavers, tanners, butchers, glassmakers, farmers, and the homeless alike were your audience. I, too, hope that my books will not be restricted to academics doing doctoral theses on Persian poetry or that they will not sit catching dust on library shelves. I want them to go into the hands and hearts of the man on the street; the man who takes the *métro* each morning and who buys his *baguette* in the *boulangerie* each evening. If the entire world can know of you, Mevlana, I will have done my job. And they will. Now, no one will ever again have to experience what I did that day in the Sorbonne library. I believe your books will one day be found on the shelves of every library in the world and that your name will be known in every land of the planet. In faraway Peru and America and China, people will read your poems in their own language and take inspiration from the path of love you paved. Pilgrims to your message will come from every corner of the world to Konya, to render homage to you, a believer in the potential of love to unite all peoples on this planet in unity with the Beloved God, with others and with themselves. They will walk past the hawkers who sell tourist trinkets, carpets, and candies and head straight to your tomb, for they know they will find there the secrets of how to live.

You have inspired us, not just by your writings, but with the example of your life. Still today, your message is of the utmost actuality, especially for the youth of the world who are hungry for a spiritual life, yet are frustrated with the ones they are living, often falling prey to marginal dogmatic sects and other poisons. Mevlana, I believe that your legacy is twofold. First, your humanism and your tenderness for others, even the most humble, is a lesson for all to emulate. Secondly, you represent the universalism of Islam and its essential spirit. You adopted a constructive ecumenical attitude towards various creeds and religions. In your daily life in Konya, you acted as a liaison between the population and the ruling class. You wrote letters to rulers appealing for justice. You showed tolerance in living with Jews and Christians, and that stance influenced the Muslim faith as it was lived at that time. You did not differentiate between religions and anyone could become part of your entourage. You remarried with a Christian woman, Kerra, who converted to Islam. You were loved by the Christian community. Your tolerance was also extended to non-believers. You often quoted the poet Sanai who said: *"Atheism and faith run together on God's path."*

You constantly advocated for tolerance, for you felt that the ritual differences used in the adoration of God were not important. There is an aspect of truth in all religions, and no matter how wide the divergences, and there is always harmony when mutual respect reigns. In fact, dogma and ritual are all too often the cause of hostility and divergence. You said that only an attachment in the most profound sense to the love of an Absolute God will be able to bring people together in a fraternal existence. Your message of universalism and love has made the *Masnavi* a work without equal in the world of Islam, and it has an important role: to shed its light to the West, for it shows us that the religion of love is the highest of all religions and communities.

Sufism is for human beings. It brings to humanity the culture of mankind. Indeed, we all live in a vast circle of love, like the *sema*, in concentric communities of hearts. You said it so beautifully in chapter 23 of the *Fihi ma Fihi*: "*There are many ways to search but the object of the search is always the same. Don't you see that the roads to Mecca are all different; one coming from Byzantium, the other from Syria, others running through land and sea? The roads are diverse, the goal, one...when the people arrive there, all quarrels, disputes, or differences of the road are resolved; they forget their differences when they arrive because there, hearts are in unison.*"

The world is now in such strife. As I write, in these blazingly hot days of July, 1999, I am chagrined to see civil wars raging in Afghanistan and Algeria with Islamic fundamentalists struggling to take power; these people who represent an Islam I cannot understand or accept. Your message has the potential to create a consciousness of community and the peace that eludes us all. I pray your words will help us lead humble lives illuminated with compassion to help preserve humanity from its own suicide at the hands of hatred, fanaticism, consumerism, fundamentalism, prejudice, wars, and the destruction of our planet and its resources!

Although I am now too weak to visit it, I often think of the sparkling white Grande Mosquée de Paris so near to my apartment. It was the first mosque I ever saw in my life, the one that was being built when I was at the start of my university years so long ago. How could I have ever imagined then what a sign it was, pointing to the rest of my life, just as the Qur'an recounts: "*We shall show them our signs in the horizons and in themselves.*" Few know that its brave *imam* Si Kaddour Bengrabit sheltered countless Jews in the mosque during the Nazi occupation of Paris during World War

II and facilitated their escape through its underground tunnels which linked to the Seine River where they could slip into a barge heading south. This is the world I wish to live in, a world where all faiths and peoples can exist in mutual respect.

Dreams have played such an important part of my life, and now, I have a dream for Islam. I dream that the plurality of Islam can find a common ground, between Sunnite, Shiite, rural, urban, and the traditional and progressive tendencies. I dream that Islam will be separated always from state governance to ensure the acceptance of the religious rights of all citizens, for Islam is a spiritual and religious authority, separate from the concerns of material and political existence. I have a dream that *ijtihad*, or the personal effort to interpret the basic texts of Islam, will prevail over a hidebound adherence to codes in texts written 1,400 years ago. I dream that priority will be placed on spirituality and values before precepts. I dream that critical thought can help find the original spiritual and universal dynamism of Islam, especially in the reading of the Meccan Qur'an as it was first written. I dream that Iqbal's hopes for a reconstruction of Islamic thought will be realized, and that man can celebrate an Islam that rejects political power and the ambition of fundamentalism. I dream that the theological dimension of Islam can help it come closer to the other Abrahamic religions of Judaism and Christianity, but also to the other religions of Buddhism, Jainism, Baha'i, Shinto, Taoism, Hinduism, and yes, agnosticism and atheism. I dream that Muslim societies can progressively move forward on a constant path towards improvement and understanding towards a humanitarian ideal in sync with the era in which we live: be it the status of women, relations with those different, service to the poor, justice for all, relations with the West, and the acceptance of scientific progress and evolving technology. I will defend your message of universalism, Mevlana, as long as I have the force within me, for it represents for me this dream I hold for our world. We can aspire to become better human beings and contribute to the common good, or we can remain caught up in our daily lives of petty concerns filled with greed, selfishness, desire for power and control. The choice is ours. This path is a long one and a hard climb, but we must all be in this together!

And now I, too, Mevlana, think about putting down my pen. My mind is still so active but my body is now completely failing me. I am so weak these days. You say: *"This world is a seedbed for the next world"* and I am now ready to harvest the grain of my life for this next world. As much as I fear death, I know it is near. Over the past year I have watched my body melt away into nothingness. I have intolerable pains on many days, and then, if by magic, there are days of total ease. I can no longer leave this apartment, or even rise from this bed. Yet, I can leave this world now, in peace. My sons are now all grown and settled in their careers; one a famous doctor and another a prosperous lawyer. What more could a mother want? I have translated your words into French, a gift I leave to this exquisitely precise language and to its speakers all around the world. What more could a scholar aspire to? Yet I still wonder if I have done enough. I have so many questions about death – it is inevitable, that I know – but I ponder the destiny of man in the Absolute. I reread, over and over, the lecture that Iqbal gave on death. He said that God created man with the confidence that he could achieve his potential and that hell is nothing more than the non-accomplishment of this divine trust. I ask myself constantly: have I earned the confidence bestowed upon me by God when He created me? Hell is not doing what you should have done as a human being, and I cannot stop asking myself if I have done enough. Have I built enough bridges, helped as many students as I could to advance, taken the right steps to charity to those near to me and to fraternity to mankind, shared more, given more, written more? I certainly have tried to do my best.

I am not alone, for my sweet companion Aïcha comes and takes care of me most days. She tends to me with the love of a mother for a newborn child. My body even looks like a newborn child now, so small and fragile. With each delicious sweet mint tea that she prepares for me, I think of all that I have learned from Sidi Hamza, my students, my colleagues, my literary and intellectual heroes, and, above all, from your verses. I try to keep positive and I even told Faouzi when he telephoned me last week that I wanted to write another book with him, but I know that this will not be possible, but I must not let him know that.

There is one thing that I wish above all. It is my most sincere wish to lie in your shadow, in the holy city of Konya, to rest there until the Judgment Day under the shadow of your blessing. I expressed this wish on my trip to your city last year to Abdullah, the tender student from Konya whom I adopted as my spiritual son, and I know he will do what he can to make this happen for me. I dream of a grave perfumed with beds of the roses of the Prophet and the lavender of the fields of my native France. Perhaps a small tree to provide shade to my weary bones, and that is enough. No fancy tomb, just a stone marker in the Üçler Cemetery, there, in the blue shade of your domed tomb, whose turquoise brilliance will light my path to the springtime of paradise and to all the skies of the Universe. You turned black ink into bright light; my ink flowed in your shadow. Now I pray I will be able to sleep in your shadow in Konya, behind your sun that now illuminates the entire world.

You say: *"I didn't come here of my own accord, and I can't leave that way. Whoever brought me here will have to take me home."* And now as I lie here in my bed, I ask myself, where is home for me? Paris, Morocco, Konya, or other? One thing is certain: wherever home is for me, you are there at my side. Mevlana, you have said that the circular dance of the *sema* is the secret of origin and return, a dance that invites us to return with serenity to the place we have come from. Death will be beautiful and light, like the movement of a dance which carries us higher. I will hold onto the image of this light when I am seized by moments of terror and pain.

I turn my head and stare at the blinding patches of light made by the brilliant summer sun reflecting off my parquet floor. Those patches remind me that light has been at my side since the first day I read you until this day when I am so very, very tired. My whole life – my choices, my research and my work – have been dedicated to the quest for the Absolute and all has fused into one large lesson that I as a teacher leave to this world. That lesson is the path to love that you have taught me Mevlana, the path that has shown me that only that which comes from the heart can open the heart. May the lesson of love that the ink of your pen turned into light never extinguish and shine forever.

We must all live together as one world. *We have so much to say to each other –*

Author's Note

Konya, 1987

Front row, Eva (age 78) and behind her, second from the right, is her spiritual son from Konya, Abdullah Öztürk

I never had the opportunity to meet Eva de Vitray-Meyerovitch, but as a young student, I, like so many others, discovered Mevlana through her writings. I lived in France pursuing a degree in Islamic Art at the same time as she was translating the *Masnavi*, and I could have been one of those students climbing the five flights of stairs to her home. I often wonder if she was in the theater the same night I attended a performance of Peter Brook's adaptation of Attar's *The Conference of the Birds* in 1979, or whether she was the tiny, grey-haired lady who used to sit next to me when I would do research in the Bibliothèque Nationale, or whether she bought her .clementines from the same greengrocer as I did on the rue Mouffetard. Perhaps yes, perhaps no, but what is certain is that this diminutive Parisian dervish made possible for the words of one of the supreme poets of humanity to turn in the hearts of so many others.

Eva de Vitray-Meyerovitch died on July 24, 1999, and was buried in a private ceremony in the Muslim sector of the cemetery of Thiais (Val de Marne) in the suburbs of Paris. Her passing went largely unnoticed, with only a brief obituary appearing in the newspapers *Le Monde* and *Libération*.

At her death in 1999, Eva had published over 40 works on Mevlana, Sufism, and Islam, including translations from English and Persian into French, original works, contributions to collective works and numerous journal and press articles. Her dedication to Mevlana brought to life for the West an unsuspected rich spiritual tradition: she accomplished complete translations of the *Masnavi* and the *Fihi ma Fihi* and partial translations of the *Divan-i Kebir* and the *Rubaiyat*. Her translations of Mevlana opened a window of understanding not only for the Christian West, but also exerted an influential impact on francophone Muslims of North Africa. Mevlana was virtually unknown outside of the Persian and Turkish sphere, including North and sub-Saharan Africa, so an entire generation of French-speaking Muslims discovered this superlative voice of their tradition via her work. She fostered a new generation of Islamic and Sufi scholars now working in countries all over the world. She helped countless young people, Muslims and Christians alike, come to a better understanding of their traditions and spiritual aspirations.

In 1994, her protégé, Faouzi Skali, created the Fez World Sacred Music Festival in Fez, Morocco, which brings together each year performers from every corner of the world for a week of artistic fellowship in this ancient holy city. He also founded in 2007 the annual Festival of Sufi Culture.

In 2007, largely due to the recognition Mevlana received in the Western world via her work, UNESCO declared 2007 "The Year of Mevlana." The *sema,* which has come down to us as one of the most deeply moving ceremonies on the planet, was inscribed on the UNESCO "Intangible Cultural Heritage of Humanity" list in 2008.

In 2008, nine years after her death, due to the resolute efforts of over five years by her "spiritual son" from Konya, Prof. Dr. Abdullah Öztürk, working in compassionate alliance with the Municipality of Konya, the remains of Eva de Vitray-Meyerovitch were transferred from the Cemetery of Thiais to Konya. As per her wishes expressed to Dr. Öztürk and others, she was re-buried in a moving ceremony in the Üçler Cemetery in the shadow of the Green Tomb of Mevlana on Wednesday, December 17, 2008, at the moment of the annual celebrations of the *Şeb-i-Arus*, the "Wedding Night" of red skies when Mevlana died and rejoined his Beloved God. *Hawwa Hanim*, as she is known by all in Konya, is the only contemporary European citizen resting in this cemetery. Her grave is visited each year by many foreign and Turkish visitors.

In 2011, a private Muslim school, recognized by the French Ministry of Education, was established in Mantes-la-Jolie in the suburbs of Paris (Yvelines). Open to all faiths, this school has over 100 students and is growing each year. Classes are offered in French and Arabic, with an option for religious instruction. The school is named l'Ecole Eva de Vitray.

The *zaviyeh* of Sheikh Boutchichi is still welcoming Sufi seekers from around the world to Morocco. Sheikh Boutchichi passed away in January, 2017, at the age of 95.

The *Masnavi* continues to be translated from the Persian into English, with several full and partial translations appearing in the last ten years. In addition to the academic translations done directly from the Persian, countless popular versions of selections from the *Masnavi* are appearing daily in English, offering a more free-handed rendering based on the translations of others. These colorful and appealing books make Mevlana's verse more easily understandable to modern ears, and have done much to make him a household name, and one who currently bears the title of bestselling poet in America – not insignificant for a man living far away in Seljuk-era Konya, Turkey, 750 years ago.

The *Masnavi*, one of the sacred books of humanity, has now been translated into 22 languages as diverse as Turkmen, Spanish, Arabic, German, Italian, Albanian, Swedish, Urdu, Japanese, Bosnian, Dutch, Kazakh, Uzbek, Tajik, Chinese, and Greek. Translations into Malaysian and Russian are currently underway. The Municipality of Konya has set a goal to reach 50 languages in the upcoming years. Many of these translations are not worked from the original Persian, but are based on the translation done by Eva de Vitray-Meyerovitch. One half of the world's population can now read this masterpiece of world literature thanks to this dynamic translation program.

The Association of the Friends of Eva de Vitray-Meyerovitch in Paris, founded to honor the memory of this exceptional woman, hosts lectures and interfaith dialogue sessions several times each year and encourages discovery of the "Other Face" of Islam, the one she so passionately promoted.

In 2014, 15 years after her death, a new collection of unpublished essays and lectures by Eva de Vitray-Meyerovitch was published in France, entitled *L'Universalité de l'Islam*. The influence of her teaching, writing, and translations is still felt more than ever.

The French translation of the *Masnavi* by Eva de Vitray-Meyerovitch originally published by the Editions du Rocher has never gone out of print, and continues to sell hundreds of copies each year. The *Masnavi* was re-edited by Rocher in 2013 and, in November, 2015, an electronic e-book version was made available.

Although she was lauded with honorary degrees and awards in Egypt, Turkey, and Pakistan, her work remained fairly unrecognized in France during her lifetime. Her atypical profile, independence, and courage to travel a path outside accepted practices of society kept her on the fringes of intellectual circles, yet this exceptional and open-minded woman never wavered in her profound desire to use the beauty of the French language to convey the most subtle points of the Islamic faith in order to touch all who sought to discover the crossroads of viewpoints. Now, almost twenty years after her death, her legacy is coming to the forefront, at a time when more people of her dimension are needed to dispel the ghosts of suspicion, fear, and misunderstanding. In a world becoming more and more haunted by the absurd and which has lost much of the sense of sacred and the quest for values, her legacy reverberates more than ever. The two tragic terrorist events in Eva de Vitray-Meyerovitch's Paris in 2015 have shown the imperative of listening to her voice, the one that shows the other face of Islam, its true face; the one that inspired her life until the very last drop of ink in her pen.

Katharine Branning
Paris, March, 2017

KATHARINE BRANNING is Vice-President of the French Institute Alliance Française in New York City, where she serves as the Director of FIAF's Library. She was awarded the Ordre National du Mérite from the President of France in 2006, one of the nation's highest honors. Ms. Branning is a graduate of the Ecole du Louvre in Paris, where she majored in Islamic arts, with a specialty in Islamic glass. As an independent researcher, she has conducted annual field work in Turkey since 1978 and is the author of a website on the Seljuk caravanserai of Turkey, www.turkishhan.org, created in 2001. She is the curator of *The Song of Stones*, the first exhibit dedicated to Seljuk art in the United States, inaugurated in New York in 2011.

Her collection of essays on Turkey, "*Yes, I would love another glass of tea*," published in 2010, has been translated and published in four languages. She is English editor of two works on Seljuk art, both published under the auspices of the Office of the President of Turkey. She is the author of a historical novel, *Moon Queen*, based on the life Mahperi Hatun, the wife of the Seljuk Sultan Alaeddin Keykubad, which was published in Turkish and English in 2014. For her work in the promotion of Turkish tea, the city of Rize, Turkey, bestowed an honorary citizenship to her in 2012, the first time in its history that a foreigner was so honored by the city. She lives in New York City.

Timeline of Eva de Vitray and Mevlana

SEMA	EVA	MEVLANA	SPIRITUAL CONCEPT
part 1: Ceremonial Entry *The dervish is ready to begin*	1909-1913 Ages 0-4 -Birth in Boulogne, France -Early childhood memories -A beloved grandmother -A privileged background	1207-1211 Ages 0-4 -Birth in Afghanistan -Family background -Scholar father: Bahaeddin Valad -Grandmother	-be truthful to yourself and others
part 2: Recital of the Nat poem *The dervish is ready to listen*	1913-1926 Ages 5-17 -Early years at school -World War I -An inquisitive mind -*Les bonnes soeurs* and stricture	1212-1222 Ages 5-15 -Early education at the feet of Bahaeddin -Departure from Balkh -Fear of Mongol invasion -On the route of exile; travels in Muslim lands: Nishapur, Samarkand, Damascus -Family settles at last in Karaman, Turkey	-the slate of knowledge must be wiped clean to learn
part 3: Ney Flute Improvisation *The dervish is ready to yearn*	1927-1940 Ages 18-30 -University studies -Breaks from the Catholic Church -Earns a law degree -Marriage to Lazare Meyerovitch -Discovery of the philosophy of Plato -Birth of 1st son	1223-1232 Ages 16-25 -Life in Karaman, marriage to Gevher -Birth of two sons -Invitation to Bahaeddin Valad by Seljuk Sultan Alaeddin Keykubad to come teach in the capital of Konya -Death of Bahaeddin Valad -Arrival of Seyyid Burhaneddin to Konya to instruct Mevlana -Study abroad in Aleppo, Syria -Returns to Konya and begins to teach in the medrese	-parallels of Plato with concepts of Sufism: -anamnesis -*Theoria* done in degrees like a latter -life is but a reflection of the true reality

Part 4: Peshrev + Drum Solo and HU!	1940-1945 Ages 30-36	-Fear of annihilation by Mongols	-love and forgiveness
The dervish is ready to submit	-Administers the research lab of Frédéric and Irène Joliot-Curie -World War II -Exile and survival		
Part 5: Sultan Veled walk	1946-1953 Ages 37-44		-definitions: Sufism, *tawhid, tarika, haqiqa, tassawif, faqir*, dervish, *sharia, marifa* -basic principles of living the Sufi way
The dervish is ready to flow	-Rebuilds life after war -Begins working at the CNRS -Birth of second son -Starts doctorate on Plato -Discovers Iqbal -Life takes a turn		
Part 6: 1st *Selam*: I acknowledge God	1954 Age 45	1232-1244 Ages 25-37	
The dervish is ready to turn	-Begins to investigate Islam -Study of Christian exegesis -Death of husband -Mentor Louis Massignon -Conversion to Islam	-Death of wife Gevher -Remarriage to Kerra -Assumes his father's teaching post in Konya -Arrival of Shams -Neglects teaching duties and family	

153

Part 7: 2nd *Selam* I praise God	1955-1968	1244-1248	-returning to the pure state of birth
	Ages 46-60	Ages 37-41	-matbah-i-sherif
			-living the Sufi life day by day
The dervish is ready to praise	-Difficulties in living as a Muslim; rejection	-Spiritual transformation at the hands of Shams	-enhancement of the Christian faith
	-Algerian War	-Disappearance of Shams and his return	-Umma
	-Continues to translate Iqbal; publishes *Reconstruction of Islamic Thought*	-Shams takes Mevlana's daughter Kimya as a bride	-the veil over reality
	-Undertakes a doctorate on Rumi	-Final disappearance of Shams	-mirror of the hidden treasure
	-Raising two sons alone	-Influence of Shams on Mevlana's poetry	-polish the mirror and the heart
	-Translation work		-unity of existence: wahdat-e wudjud
	-Brings dervishes to Paris		
	-First trip to a Muslim country: Turkey; vision in the Hamus-hane		
	-Events of May '68, defends doctoral thesis on Rumi		
Part 8: 3rd *Selam*: I submit to God	1969-73	1248	-becoming; life is a series of changes
	Ages 61-64	Age 41	-concept of time in the present moment
			-inshallah
The dervish is ready to surrender	-Teaching at Al-Azhar	-Alaeddin Keykubad creates a cultural hub in Konya	-universalism
	-Importance of teaching, Socratic method	-Teaching at the Iplikci Medrese	-love of God = religion
	-performs the Hajj	-Shams gone for good; withdraws into himself	-teaching by fable
		-Writing of the Discourses in honor of Shams	-Fihi mi Fihi, Majalis-i Saba
		-Zarkoubi the goldsmith succeeds Shams	-discursive path to learning
			-description of the Hajj

Part 9: 4th *Selam*: I will serve God	1974-1984 Ages 65-75	1248-1258 Ages 41-51	-Attar's Conference of the Birds -Fana
The dervish is ready to serve	-Lecture tours, television -Writing; comparison of Islam to Western thinkers -Start of Masnavi translation -Peter Brook Conference of Birds -Hafiz in a church at Christmas -Lectures around the world -Trip to Iran -Trips to Konya -Students gather -Meets Abdullah Öztürk, adopted son	-Mongols approach the gates of Konya -Death of Zarkoubi -Founding of tariqas	-elimination of nafs -die before you die -climb the ladder to perfection -tariqas of brotherhood -service to others
Part 10: Qur'an reading	1985-1990 Ages 76-80	1248-1258 Ages 41-51	-necessity of a sheikh as a spiritual guide -practice of dhikr -5 pillars of Islam
The dervish is ready to honor	-Meets Faouzi Skali -Sufi studies with Sheikh Al-Boutchichi in Morocco	-Establishes the *sema* -Legend of the hammer tapping in Zarkoubi's workshop -Early women followers	-definitions: tariqa, zaviyeh, murshid, murid, silsila, sir, tawhid, wadifa, tespih, hal, dhikr, sheikh, irada, baraka

Part 11: Niyaz Farewell Prayers *The dervish is ready to pray*	1990 Age 81 -Publication of the translation of the Masnavi at age 80 -Translation challenges -Fatigue and illness	1262-1273 Ages 55-66 -Husamuddin Çelebi -Begins dictating the Masnavi to Husamuddin	-Masnavi: description and content -Adab and erkan -fables -signs and symbols
Part 12: final: departure of the Postnishin *The dervish is ready to love*	1991-1999 Ages 86-90 -Becomes ill -Prayer book -Jesus book -Hopes for the future of Islam -Desire to be buried at Konya -Death	1262-1273 Ages 55-66 -Finishes dictating the Masnavi -Death of Rumi -Funeral of Rumi -Son Valad codifies the *Sema* and lodges -Mevlevi dervish lodges set up around the world -Sultan Valad leads the Mevlevi movement	-prayer in Islam -Jesus in Islam -legacy of Rumi

Glossary of Terms

adab. The code of etiquette and courtesy the dervishes show toward their spiritual guide, toward each other, toward other people in general – as well as to themselves.

Allah. The Arabic word for God. The God with no equal, partner, sons, or daughters; the Lord of all beings, who sent messengers (*resul*), known and unknown, to all peoples at all times.

Attar, Farid-ud Din. Persian Sufi poet from Nishapur (c. 1145-1221), especially known for *The Conference of the Birds.*

aynel yaqin. "Eye of Certainty," or having a glimpse of Divine Reality; knowledge gained by seeing oneself clearly

Bahaeddin Valad. Mevlana's father, an Islamic scholar and preacher, presumably born in Balkh, the former Khorasan (the actual northwest Iran, southern Turkmenistan and northern Afghanistan), around 1152.

baqa-billah. A Sufi term which refers to essential subsistence following the experience of "mystical death," or the passing away or "annihilation" of ego (*fana*).

baraka. The blessings and grace that flows from God into creation. It is especially concentrated in saints and holy places.

Beautiful Names (*asmayi hüsna*). In Islam there is a tradition that God has ninety-nine Beautiful Names and Attributes. Most of them are found in the Qur'an. They are often chanted by Sufis and repeated (generally with a *tespih* in hand), so one can try to live the blessing of that attribute.

Beloved. God, the Absolute. Never means a sweetheart or lover.

Bismillah ir-rahman ir-rahim. "In the name of God, the Most Merciful, the Most Compassionate": the most used phrase of blessing in Islam. It is often said at the beginning of any important action. It precedes all the chapters but one (the Taubah) in the Qur'an.

dervish. The Persian word for a Sufi, the same as *faqir*. It is a common word used to denote a Sufi.

destegül. The short jacket with sleeves to the wrists which is worn over the "whirling skirt" (*tennure*) during the *sema*.

devr-i kebir. The Sufi practice of doing *dhikr* while whirling. In a number of Islamic cultures and Sufi orders there have been dervishes who felt so moved by their love of God, that they began to whirl. The *devr-i kebir* is the term for the Mevlevi music in the *sema.*

dhikr. "Remembrance of God": refers to the Islamic Sufi practice of repeating sacred words, the Divine Name or phrases in Arabic, either out loud or silently, individually, or in a group. Common *dhikrs* are *"lâ illâha illâ 'llâh"* (there is no divinity but God) and "Allah, Allah! (the traditional Mevlevi *dhikr*).

Divan-e Kebir. "The Mystical Odes"; also known as the *Divan-e Shams-I Tabrizi.* A *divan* is a collection of poetry. This is the second major work of poetry by Mevlana and is named in honor of his master Shams and in which he expresses mystical love. In addition to approximately 35,000 Persian couplets and 2,000 Persian quatrains, the Divan contains 90 *ghazals* (a short poem of between ten and fifteen verses) and 19 quatrains in Arabic, a couple of dozen or so couplets in Turkish (or mixed Persian and Turkish) and 14 couplets in Greek.

dua. A personal supplication, which may be said in any language, silently or aloud (often verses in Arabic from the Qur'an or prayers of the Prophet Muhammad), usually with the hands raised up facing the heavens. They are recited to ask a request of God, such as for forgiveness, healing, or help. At the conclusion, the fingers of both hands are gently wiped over the face (in hopes of receiving blessing from the prayer). It is different from the ritual formal prayer, composed of *rakats*, or cycles of prayer and movement (standing, bowing, prostration).

elif-named. The long cloth belt worn by the dervishes during the *sema.*

erkan. Rules of conduct on the Sufi path.

ezan. (In Arabic: *adhan*) The Islamic call to prayer, an announcement made in a loud voice from a mosque five times daily by the *muezzin.*

fana. The annihilation of the egotistical self. The final state of fana is the *fana fillah*, when one is no longer conscious of having attained *fana.*

faqir. "Poor" or "Empty": The most common Arabic term used to mean a Sufi, in the sense that one is "poor and needy in front of God" and aiming to be empty of all but His presence. We are beggars for the grace of God. The Persian word for *faqir* is darwish, which has become the term "dervish."

Fatiha. The Opening chapter of the Qur'an (1: 1-7), containing seven short lines: *"In the name of God the Most Merciful, the All-Compassionate. Praise is to God, the Sustaining Lord of all the worlds, the All-Merciful, the Most Compassionate, Owner of the Day of Judgment. Only you do we serve and only You do we ask for help. Guide us on the path most straight, the path of those upon whom You have given blessing; other than the path of those upon whom is Your condemnation, and not the path of those who go astray."* It is the prayer most often recited in Islam, said many times daily, always standing, especially at the start of the ritual prayer prior to bowing. It is silently recited several times by the *semazens* during the *sema*.

Fihi ma Fihi. *"What's in It is in It."* A prose work in Persian (with two discourses in Arabic), consisting of excerpts from 71 of Mevlana's lectures and courses compiled by his students after his death. The style of the *Fihi ma Fihi* is colloquial and meant for middle-class men and women, and as such is the most accessible of Mevlana's works.

gülbanki. "The Song of the Rose": a short prayer blessing holy personages of the past who are part of the Mevlevi lineage, intoned in solemn Persian by a leader following a meal, the *sema* and on other occasions.

hadith. The recorded sayings or deeds of the Prophet Muhammad as related by his companions down through a chain of narrators. Together with the Qur'an, the *hadiths* constitute the jurisprudence from which the *sharia* is drawn. Also known as *sunnah*.

hafiz. Title given to one who learns the Qur'an by heart. Traditionally, this learning starts in childhood in Qur'anic schools.

hajj. The great pilgrimage to Mecca, the Fifth Pillar of the Faith. The man or woman who accomplishes it is known as a *hajji/hajja*.

hal. A brief spiritual state or mystic experience of peace, love, and awe at the majesty of God, like flashes of lightning, as opposed to the longer spiritual station of *maqam*.

hamdam. Persian for "being of the same breath": the complicity and deep love shared between the *Sheikh* and his students.

hamushane. Persian "house of the silent ones"; it is the name for the cemetery next to a Mevlevi dervish lodge (*Mevlevihane*) where dervishes are buried.

haq-al yaqin. The "Truth of Certainty" or knowledge gained through direct experience with God.

haqiqa. "The truth of God." The inner, esoteric reality of all that is created, of all law, of all religion. It is the spiritual "straight path" towards God, as opposed to the "wide path" of the law (*sharia*).

haqq. One of the Names or Attributes of God, which refers to the Truth or Divine Reality.

haqq-dost. Persian word for "Friend of the Truth"

hat-i istiva. In the *sema*, there is an invisible straight line conceived as extending from the Sheikh's sheepskin (*post*) in front of the *mihrab*. The *semazens* are to avoid stepping on this straight line, out of respect. The *Sheikh* (*postnishin*), however, may walk directly on the invisible line during the ceremony, as well as when entering and exiting the *semahane*, which signifies that he is the guide who understands the straight path to Divine Reality for the dervishes.

Hawwa. The Arabic word for the name Eva.

HaZret. An honorific title (*Hz*) which precedes the names of holy personages, akin to "His Holiness", and referring to Divine presence.

hu. The greatest Name of God.

Husamuddin Chelebi. Mevlana's favorite disciple, who became his closest spiritual companion after Salah al-din Zarkub died in 1258. He was appointed to teach and train disciples. Husamuddin was the one who asked Mevlana to compose a *masnavi* (book of rhymed couplets), and the one who wrote down the verses of the *Masnavi* as they were dictated by Mevlana.

ihram. The plain white cotton attire worn by all pilgrims in Mecca.

ilm al yaqin. "Knowledge of certainty" or Knowing something about Divine Reality; knowledge gained through study.

imam. Islamic spiritual leader of the community. The person who leads prayers, and, if well-educated, the equivalent to a rabbi in Judaism.

insan-i kamil. "Perfect" or "Universal" Man. A term used to denote a fully realized and complete human being. An important theme in the work of the Sufi Ibn Arabi.

inshallah. The Arabic expression for "If God wills it." It is traditional for Muslims to add this phrase when speaking about the future.

Islam. Submission to the Will of God. Since the word "*salaam*" means "peace and security," the word "islam" can be understood to mean the way to peace and tranquility by submission to the Will of God. In contrast to the filial (Father-child) relationship of Christianity, in Islam the relationship between God and human beings is viewed as being that of Lord and servant; a reminder that Islam means the submission of one's whole being to divine will.

Jelaleddin. "Glory of the Religion." It was the nickname given to Mevlana as a child by his father, Bahaeddin Valad.

jihad. Etymologically, the word *Jihad* means "effort", "fight" or "struggle." It is used to denote the internal struggle against the selfish soul in order to become a good Muslim.

Kaaba. From the Arabic word for "cube." The cube-shaped sanctuary in Mecca, towards which all Muslims pray. It stands on the place where the Prophet Abraham and his son Ishmael are believed to have built the first sanctuary to worship the One True God. In Mecca, there are always pilgrims engaged in a ritual counter-clockwise circumambulation (*tawaf*) walking prayer around the Kaaba, day and night, every day of the year.

kanun. A zither-like stringed instrument used in the *sema* ceremony, played horizontally with the fingers.

kemançe. A type of violin used in the *sema* ceremony.

khalwat. A solitary retreat, traditionally for 40 days, during which a Sufi disciple does extensive spiritual exercises under the direction of a Sufi *sheikh*. (*Halvet* in Turkish).

khirka. A long black cloak with very long sleeves and no collar or buttons worn during the *sema*. It symbolizes the grave of the *dervish*.

kudum. A small double drum played with small sticks during the *sema*. The chief drum player (*kudümzenbashi*) decides the tempo of the various musical sections.

Majalis-e Saba. "*The Seven Sessions*": A collection of seven Friday sermons by Mevlana, in Persian with introductory prayers in Arabic for each sermon. The sermons themselves give a commentary on the deeper meaning of Qur'an and Hadith. The style of Persian is rather simple, but the quotation of Arabic, historical references and the Hadith show Mevlana's knowledge of the Islamic sciences.

Makatib. "*The Letters*" is the book containing Mevlana's letters in Persian to his disciples, family members, and men of state (Vizier Suleiman Pervane in particular). *The Letters* indicate that Mevlana was busy helping family members and administering a community of disciples that had grown up around him. The letters are sophisticated in style, which is in conformity with the expectations of correspondence directed to nobles and states-

directed to nobles and statesmen.

maqamat. Stages on the Sufi path towards knowledge of God. It is increasing awareness acquired through individual effort of love, and are permanent and not temporary stations.

marifa. "The knowing of God." Spiritual knowledge, an ongoing state of attunement with God and with truth. *Marifa* is the final of the four stages of Sufism: *Sharia, Tariqa, Haqiqa,* and *Marifa.* It is the station of knowledge achieved by saints and Prophets.

Masnavi. A rhyming couplet. Specifically, the *Masnavi* is the name of the poetic masterpiece of Mevlana's last years, composed in six books, consisting of 25,700 rhymed couplets in Persian. It is a compendium of Sufi and ethical teachings, and is deeply permeated with Qur'anic meanings and references, as well as many sayings (*hadith*) of the Prophet Muhammad. It is considered by many to be one of the greatest works of mystical poetry.

matbah-i sheref. The Sufi kitchen. In the Mevlevi tradition, food was prepared with much spiritual concentration and remembrance of God. Novices must spend a 1001 day retreat working in the kitchen to learn humility and how to become a *dervish.*

medrese. An institution of higher education in the Islamic world. Mevlana taught in the Iplikçi Medrese in Konya, Turkey.

Merace-Bahreyn. The place in Konya where it is believed that Mevlana met Shams-i Tabrizi. It is a pilgrimage place for Mevlevis.

Mevlana. Literally "Our Master", the title given to Jelaleddin Muhammad al-Balkhi (known in the West as "Rumi"), the author of the *Masnavi.* He lived from 1207 to 1273.

Mevlevi. The Islamic Sufi order which is based on the teachings and traditions of Mevlana. It was first organized in the Seljuk era by his son Sultan Valad and his grandson Arif Chelebi to carry on his teachings, and continued on through the Ottoman period until 1925 when it was deemed illegal in secular Turkey. It is known in the West as the Whirling Dervishes.

mihrab. The niche in a wall or pillar of a mosque which indicates the direction of prayer which always must face toward Mecca. In the *sema,* it is customary to place the red sheepskin (*post*) upon which the *Sheikh* sits, in front of the *mihrab.*

Miraj. The miraculous night journey made by the Prophet Muhammad from Mecca to Jerusalem and then ascension through the seven heavens.

Mongols. Tribes from the Mongolian region of China who swept west in the 13th century under the command of Genghis Khan and later his grandsons. They were a constant threat to all in their destructive path. The Seljuks were defeated by them in 1243, after which they became their vassals.

mosque. (*masjid* in Arabic): An Islamic building dedicated to the performance of the five daily prayers, the weekly Friday congregational sermon and prayer, and other religious obligations and gatherings.

muezzin. The one who calls Muslims to pray, by saying the Call to Prayer (*ezan*) in a loud voice, traditionally from the *minaret* (tower) of a mosque. In modern times, he has been generally replaced by a recording played on a PA system affixed to the *minaret.*

Muhammad. The messenger of God, who received the Revelation called the "Qur'an" via the angel Gabriel. He was born in Mecca, according to tradition in the year 570, and died in Medina, Arabia in 632. The Holy Qur'an states clearly that he is the final Messenger of God to be sent to earth before the second coming of Jesus at the end of this cycle of time (Qur'an 33:40).

muhur. In the *sema*, the humble standing position in front of the *Sheikh* in which the right big toe is placed on top of the left big toe. The other parts are crossing the right arm over the left with hands on shoulders, head held downwards to the left, and eyes looking downward.

mukabele. From the Arabic word meaning "facing another." It is another name for the *sema*, because the participants face and bow to each other during the first part of the ceremony (the Sultan Valad Cycle), and face God, the Only Beloved, during the *sema*.

murid. Student; the disciple of a Sufi master or guide.

murshid. The Sufi master, teacher and spiritual guide of a Sufi disciple (*murid*). Also called the *Sheikh, pir,* or *dede.*

Muslim. One who submits to the will of God is a "muslim." It means one who honors God by following the religious way that was revealed to the Prophet Muhammad through the Qur'an.

mutribhane. In the *sema*, the balcony room in which the musicians (*mutrib*) play their instruments and sing, opposite the *mihrab*, in front of which the *Sheikh* stands and sits on his sheepskin (*post*).

nafs. Variously defined as the bodily self or the narcissistic ego. A major part of the spiritual work of Sufism is learning to combat the lower self until it submits to the Divine Will and becomes pleasing to God. *Nafs* is frequently described as having seven levels, from base existence through complete purity.

1.   The Selfish Self: people at this level follow the basic functions of life, like animals: they grow, breathe, eat, and digest. The soul is dominated by selfishness and with no sense of morality or compassion, and is filled only with physical and egotistical desires.

2.   The Regretful Self: At this stage people begin to become conscious of their self-centered tendencies and the effects they have on their lives. Wants and desires still dominate; the person repents from time to time and tries to follow higher impulses, but does not yet have the ability to change.

3.   The Inspired Self: the state where the individual begins to experience the joys of prayer, worship, and meditation; however, selfish thoughts are still present. Now the seeker is motivated by ideals such as compassion, service, and higher moral values. This is the beginning of the real practice of Sufism.

4.   The Tranquil Self: the seeker is now at peace and serene. At this point individuals are content with their lives and do not strive for more wealth, fame, or pleasure. The struggles of the earlier stages are basically over. The egotistical self begins to let go, allowing the individual to come more closely in contact with the Divine.

5.   The Contented Self: at this stage, the individual is not only content with his or her lot, but is pleased even when faced with the difficulties and trials of life, realizing that they are spiritual opportunities which have come from God.

6.   The Harmonious Self: those who reach this stage realize that all power to act comes from God, and they can do nothing by themselves. They no longer fear anything or ask for anything and have achieved genuine inner unity.

7.   The Pure Self: those few – this is the realm of the Saints and the Prophets – who attain the final level have transcended the self entirely. At this stage, the completed individual has truly realized the truth that "There is no god but God."

namaz. The Islamic ritual prayer, done by Muslims five times a day: prior to sunrise, just past noon, late afternoon, just after sunset, and following the end of twilight. The prayer includes the postures of standing, bowing, and prostrating. Before praying, one must wash the hands, face, arms, and feet with water, according to the Islamic requirement for purification. It is also one of the "Five Pillars of Islam" (*shahada*, fasting during *Ramazan*, an annual 2.5% almsgiving to charity and pilgrimage to Mecca once in a lifetime for those who can afford it.)

nat-i sherif. A *nat* is a eulogy of praise; the *sema* begins with this "noble eulogy" of the singing of the praises of the Prophet Muhammad.

ney. A reed flute, with nine holes (a thumb hole, six finger holes, and the top and bottom openings). It is played by the *neyzan* during the *sema* and is the main symbol in the first eighteen lines of the *Masnavi.*

niyaz. The neediness of a *dervish* before God. This is a major teaching of Mevlana. The *dervish* must increase his or her neediness in order to receive Divine blessings and greater nearness to God. The word also is used to mean the humble physical position called *muhur,* as well as the modest manner in which a *dervish* greets his superior or in which one *dervish* would greet another.

nur. Universal Light which touches every part of the universe, divine light.

peshrev. A prelude or first section in classical Turkish music. In the *sema,* it is the music composed for the Sultan Valad cycle.

post. A red sheepskin upon which the *Sheikh* stands and sits during the *sema.* It symbolizes his authority and other meanings, such as the sacrifice of the lower self or ego *(nafs).* The red color symbolizes the manifestation of God *(tajalli)* to the prophets and saints. It also symbolizes the sunset at the time of Mevlana's death, as well as a symbol of Shams. It is traditionally placed in front of the *mihrab,* indicating the direction of Mecca.

postnishin. The Mevlevi *Sheikh* who stands and sits on the red sheepskin *(post)* and who is the leader of the *sema.* He symbolizes the presence of Mevlana.

qasida. A type of Arabic poetry that can often be sung as a sort of hymn.

qibla. The direction, toward the Kaaba in Mecca, which all Muslims face while doing the ritual prayers five times a day.

qidam. "Rank": Mevlevis are ranked according to how long ago they were initiated as Mevlevis (and not according to age) and sit in rank accordingly. In the *sema,* the whirler *(semazen)* with the most seniority is the first in line to whirl.

Qur'an. From the Arabic word meaning "recitation", it is the holy scripture revealed in Arabic to the Prophet Muhammad from God, through the archangel Gabriel, over a period of 23 years.

It was compiled into a single book shortly after Muhammad's death by the order of the first Caliph, Abu Bakr. It comprises 114 chapters (*suras*), varying in length from 3 lines to 286 lines. The Qur'an presents itself not as a completely new message, but as a reconfirmation of the essential message given by God to all the previous prophets, from Noah and Abraham to Moses and Jesus.

qutb. "Pole" in Arabic. The center of the circle of *dervishes* during the *sema.*

Ramadan. The Islamic month of fasting (from food, water, sex, tobacco, anger, and impure thoughts) from sunrise to sunset. It is one of the five pillars of Islam. The Prophet Muhammad first began to receive the Revelation of the Qur'an during this month.

rebab. A short-necked lute played in the *sema*, with two strings made of horse hair, played upright.

resul. A prophet of God who has been given a message for mankind. These messengers, sent by God throughout history, can be unknown or can be those of other scriptures, such as Jesus, Moses, and Abraham.

Rumi. The term Rumi is derived from the Latin word for Rome, or "Roman", or one who dwells in the Eastern Roman Byzantine land of Anatolia. It is the name by which Mevlana is most often called in Europe and America. He is not called "Rumi" in Muslim countries, where he is referred to more respectfully as Mevlana. He spent most of his life in Anatolia (now known as Turkey) and died on December 17, 1273.

salat. The Arabic word for canonical prayer. A ritual prayer recital during the *sema.*

Şeb-i arus. The Persian word for "wedding night." It refers to the night when Mevlana died (and became "wedded" to God, the Beloved). A special *sema* is observed on the anniversary of this night (December 17 on the Western solar calendar). It is a moment of intense pilgrimage to Konya from *dervishes* from all over the world.

selam. Literally, "greeting of peace." In the *sema*, this word refers to the four separate vocal musical sections, each of which has different music composed for it, as well as a different spiritual characteristic.

Seljuks. The name of the first Turkish Dynasty that ruled in Anatolia, from c. 1000 to 1307. It was a period of cultural development in the arts, architecture, and religious thought, especially under Sultan Alaeddin Keykubad (1220-1237). Their capital was in Konya, where Mevlana lived for the greater part of his life.

sema. A spiritual exercise done in Sufi gatherings, involving spontaneous physical movement and motions inspired by listening to recitations of the Qur'an, Sufi poetry, music, and songs, in which the *dervishes* enter an ecstatic state of spiritual consciousness. In the Mevlevi tradition, this became formalized into a ritual of disciplined whirling called the *sema*, or the Whirling Prayer Ceremony, accompanied by musicians and poetry recitations, composed mainly by Mevlana, his son, and grandson. It should not be considered as "dancing," or a stage show, as it is intended to be a form of sacred concentrated prayer.

semahane. The building, large hall or room where the *sema* is done.

semazen. Someone who is trained to turn as a "whirler" in the Whirling Prayer Ceremony. The *semazen* whirls with the left foot solidly on the floor; the right foot touches the floor after a complete circle, pointing toward the center of the circle, and stepping according to the beat of the music; the arms are outstretched and held upward; the right hand is opened to the sky and the left hand is turned downward. The gaze is upon the left thumb; the head is turned leftward (the direction of the heart), and bent toward the upheld right arm, all the while mentally repeating the *dhikr*, "Allah, Allah" with each step and rotation of the whirling.

semazenbashi. The leader of the *semazens,* who, after receiving permission from the *Sheikh*, silently guides the *semazens* in order to maintain a particular harmonious pattern and spacing in the *sema.*

Seyyid Burhaneddin. Mevlana's first Sufi master, who was the chief disciple of Mevlana's father. Following the death of his father, Mevlana studied with him for a period of nine years, prior to meeting Shams-i Tabrizi. Sayyid Burhaneddin sent him to Syria (Aleppo and Damascus) to study traditional Islamic learning and later ordered him to do a number of austere spiritual retreats. He died in 1240 in Kayseri.

shahada. The testimony of acceptance of the faith of Islam, which consists in acknowledging the Oneness of God and that Muhammad was an authentic Prophet sent by God. It is the first pillar of Islam and the foundation of the Muslim faith. It is said as a ritual act by someone who makes the intention to become a Muslim.

Shams-i Tabrizi. "Sun of the Religion." Mevlana's second spiritual teacher (after studying for nine years under Sayyid Burhaneddin). Originally from the city of Tabriz in Persia, he came to Konya in 1244 in search of someone worthy of sharing his mystical wisdom. He disappeared in 1248, believed by some to have been murdered. His sayings (mostly in Persian, some in Arabic) were written down by his disciples and are known as the "Discourses."

sharia. "The Law of God." The sacred Law of Islam; the "outer reality" as opposed to the "inner reality" of haqiqa. It is the "Wide Path" which is intended to guide people to act in harmony with the will of God through daily worship and by following the guidelines of proper conduct, much like the Ten Commandments. It is based upon interpretations of the Qur'an and the recorded practices (Sunnah) of the Prophet Muhammad.

Sheikh. The word for "Elder" in Arabic. A Sufi spiritual master, teacher, or guide. Also spelled shaykh. The master guide of spiritual hearts in a Sufi brotherhood. The connection between a dervish and sheikh is one of intense devotion. In the sema, he symbolizes the presence of Mevlana. Known as pir in Persian.

sikke. The tall conical or cylindrical hat worn by the semazens. It is usually made from camel's hair and colored brown, honey, or white. It symbolizes the dervish's tombstone. The Mevlevi sikke is not worn in public places outside of the semahane. Mevlevis were buried with their sikkes.

silsila. The chain or line of succession by which a Sufi order (tariqa) traces its descent from the Prophet Muhammad via an unbroken lineage passed from Sheikh to Sheikh.

sirr. The spiritual secret or innermost being.

sohbet. The conversation of a spiritual master with his disciples or guests. In Sufism, such contact is believed to be a primary means of transmission of the grace (baraka) of the spiritual master to his students, and forms the basis of the Sufi education.

son peshrev. "The Last Peshrev": In the sema, the instrumental musical section which follows the end of the fourth selam and is followed by a section called "son yürük semai" just prior to the final instrumental solo and the recitation of the Holy Qur'an.

Sufi. Possibly from the Persian word "woolen one." The term for practitioners of the mystical dimension of Islam, who apparently adopted (scratchy) woolen garments much like Christian ascetics. The word covers a wide range of types of mystics engaged in a variety of spiritual practices and attitudes. The term may also originate from the Arabic word for purity.

Sufism. School or esoteric current of Islam. Sufism (*tasawwuf*) is a composite of Islamic sciences. As a way of spiritual initiation, it is based on an inward interpretation of the religion. Its foundation is the daily worship and the guidelines and boundaries of conduct in Islam (*sharia*), and its branches are the path (*tariqa*), mystical knowledge (*marifa*), and ultimate truth (*haqiqah*).

Sultan Valad. Mevlana's son. After Mevlana's death, his first successor was his closest disciple, Husamuddin Chelebi. Sultan Valad was the second successor after Husamuddin's death. Sultan Valad is considered to be the first to begin organizing the whirling prayer (*sema*) into a structured ceremony, based on the essentials of his father's practice.

sunnah. The authentic tradition of the Prophet of Islam. It is the deeds and words (*hadith*) of the Prophet reported by his companions and compiled later into a corpus. They are recommended for Muslims to follow (some of which are considered obligatory and others voluntary).

tafsir. Commentary or critical interpretation of scripture.

tahqiq. Spiritual realization. For the adept of *tasawwuf*, it is the goal of the Way (*tariqa*) through extinction in God (*fana fillah*).

taksim. A musical solo improvised on a particular musical instrument. During the *sema*, a *ney* solo always precedes the Sultan Valad Circling. Another solo is played following the Fourth *Selam*, at which time the *postnishin* slowly returns to the *post*.

tanbur. A long-necked lute played during the *sema*.

tariqa. The way to God in Sufism. It is the path of spiritual purification and training in mystical disciplines. Its foundation is based in daily worship and by following the guidelines of proper conduct in Islam (*sharia*), leading then to the more advanced levels of mystical knowledge (*marifa*) and ultimate truth (*haqiqa*). It also denotes a specific Sufi brotherhood order, such as the Qadiriyyah, the Nakshibandi, the Rifai or the Mevlevi, within which the disciples follow a religious teaching and are attached to a master.

tasawwuf. The Arabic word for Sufism, the mystical dimension of Islam.

tawhid. Doctrine of the Divine Unity. The foundation of belief in Islam.

tef. A hand-held drum played during the *sema* ceremony.

tennure. The white dress-like garment worn by *semazens* during the
 sema. It hangs from the shoulders and floats upwards in a circle
 as the *dervishes* spin faster. The white color of this garment is
 the same color as the burial cloth for all Muslims. During the
 sema, the whirlers are trained to be in a concentrated state of
 prayer, yet remain alert to their positions in the whirling circle
 and not to let one's *tennure* knock against the one of another
 semazen.

tespih. String of 33 or 99 beads used to perform the *dhikr* exercise of
 reciting the Beautiful Names, phrases of the Qur'an or a litany
 (wird) given by one's Sheikh.

ud. A short-necked lute with six strings played during the *sema* ceremony.

umma. The global community of Muslim believers.

wadifa. The evocation of qualities of Allah by reciting or meditating
 on some or all of the 99 Names of Allah, often done as a group.

wahdat-e-wudjud. The Unity of Existence: we live as one in the world.
 Oneness of Being, the central doctrine of Sufism.

Zarkub (Salah al-din Zarkub). A fellow disciple of Mevlana's first
 Sheikh, Seyyid Burhaneddin, and then of Mevlana. After the
 final disappearance of Shams-i Tabrizi, he became Mevlana's
 closest spiritual companion. He was put in charge of teaching
 and training all the disciples, and died in 1254.

zaviyeh. It is the place where *dervishes* would meet to study, do prayer-
 chanting (*dhikr*) and receive spiritual instruction from a teacher
 (*Sheikh*). Some were simple and others had separate cells for the
 dervishes to live in, a kitchen, and an attached mosque or tomb of
 a saint. Other terms include *dergah, tekke, dervish lodge* or *khanaqah*.
 Etymologically, the term means "a corner", which symbolizes
 the meeting of the temporal and spiritual dimensions.

Bibliography of Works
by Eva de Vitray-Meyerovitch

1935. Li Chang. *Mœurs des mandarins sous la dynastie mandchoue.* Translated from the English. Paris: Payot, 1935.

1955. Iqbal, Mohammed. *Reconstruire la pensée religieuse de l'islam.* Translated from the original English and notes by Eva de Vitray-Meyerovitch. Preface by Louis Massignon. Paris: Librairie d'Amérique et d'Orient, 1955; Adrien-Maisonneuve, 1995; Monaco: Rocher, 1996.

1956. Fryzee, Asaf Ali Adghar. *Conférences sur l'Islam.* Translation by Eva de Vitray-Meyerovitch, preface by Louis Massignon. Paris: CNRS, 1956.

1956. Iqbal, Mohammed. *Message de l'Orient.* Translated from the original English by Eva de Vitray-Meyerovitch and Mohammad Achena. Paris: Société d'Edition les Belles Lettres, 1956.

1962. Iqbal, Mohammed. *Le livre de l'éternité.* Translated from the original English by Eva de Vitray-Meyerovitch, avec la collaboration de Mohammed Mokri. Paris: Albin Michel, 1962.

1964. Vitray-Meyerovitch, Eva de. *Henri VIII.* Paris: Julliard, 1964, 1972.

1968. Rees, Richard, *Simone Weil: esquisse d'un portrait.* Translated from the English by Eva de Vitray-Meyerovitch. Paris: Buchet-Chastel, 1968.

1968. Vitray-Meyerovitch, Eva de. *Thèmes mystiques dans l'œuvre de Djalal-ud-din Rumi.* Doctoral dissertation, 1968.

1972. Vitray-Meyerovitch, Eva de. *Mystique et poésie en Islam: Djalal-ud-Din Rumi et l'ordre des derviches tourneurs.* Paris: Desclée de Brouwer, 1972, 1982.

1973. Jalal-al-din Rumi Maulana. *Odes mystiques.* Translated from the Persian by Eva de Vitray-Meyerovitch and Mohammad Mokri. Paris: Klincksieck, 1973, 1984; Paris: Seuil, 2003.

1974. Zaehner, R.C. *L'Hindouisme.* Translated from the original English by Eva de Vitray-Meyerovitch. Paris: Desclée De Brouwer, 1974.

1976. Attar, Farid al-Din. *Le mémorial des saints (Taz'Kerrat al-awliya)*. Translated from the Ouigour by A. Pavet de Courteille. Preface by Eva de Vitray-Meyerovitch. Paris: Le Seuil, 1976.

1976. Jalal-al-din Rumi Maulana. *Le livre du dedans: fihi-ma-fihi*. Translated from the Persian by Eva de Vitray-Meyerovitch. Paris: Sinbad, 1976, 1989; Paris: Albin Michel, 1997; Arles: Actes Sud, 2010. Translated into Italian and Spanish.

1977. Vitray-Meyerovitch, Eva de. *Rumi et le Soufisme*. Paris: Seuil, 1977, 2001, 2005, 2015. Translated into English, Roumanian, Portuguese, Bosnian, and Czech.

1978. Vitray-Meyerovitch, Eva de. *Anthologie du soufisme*. Paris: Sinbad, 1978, 1986, 1989; Albin Michel, 1995.

1978. Vitray-Meyerovitch, Eva de. *Approche symbolique de l'écriture chez quelques mystiques musulmans*. Tunis: Université de Tunis, [1978].

1982. Vitray-Meyerovitch, Eva de. *Les Chemins de la lumière: 75 contes soufis*. Paris: Retz, 1982. Translated into Spanish.

1982. Sultan Valad. *Maître et disciple*. Translated from the original Persian by Djamchid Mortazavi and Eva de Vitray-Meyerovitch. Paris: Sinbad, 1982.

1983. Zaehner, R.C. *Mystique sacrée, mystique profane*. Translated from the original English by Eva de Vitray-Meyerovitch. Monaco: Editions du Rocher, 1983.

1984. Hirashima, Hussein Yoshio et Eva de Vitray-Meyerovitch. *La Mecque: ville sainte de l'Islam*. Paris: R. Laffont, 1984.

1984. Vitray-Meyerovitch, Eva de. *Islam, Christianisme*. Saint-Zacharie (France): Editions de l'Ouvert, 1984.

1984. Vitray-Meyerovitch, Eva de. *La Mecque: ville sainte de l'Islam*. Paris: R. Laffont, 1984. Translated into Italian, German, and Turkish.

1984. Vitray-Meyerovitch, Eva de, André Borrély, and Jean-Yves Leloup. *L'image de l'homme dans le Christianisme et l'Islam*. [Saint-Zacharie, France]: Editions de l'Ouvert, 1984.

1987. Jalal-al-din Rumi Maulana. *Rubai'yat*. Translated from the original Persian by Eva de Vitray-Meyerovitch. Paris: Albin Michel, 1987, 1993, 2003.

1988. Mortazavi, Djamchid. *Le Secret de l'unite dans l'estorisme iranien*. Preface de Eva de Vitray-Meyerovitch. Paris: Dervey, 1988.

1988. Vitray-Meyerovitch, Eva de. *Présence de l'Islam*. Konya: Selçuk Universitesi, 1988.

1988. Sultan Valad. *La Parole secrète: enseignement du maitre sou-fi Rumi.* Translated from the original Persian by Djamchid Mortazavi and Eva de Vitray-Meyerovitch. Monaco: Rocher, 1988.

1989. Iqbal, Mohammed. *Les secrets de soi, les mystères du non-moi.* Translated from the Persian by Djamchid Mortazavi and Eva de Vitray-Meyerovitch. Paris: Albin Michel, 1989.

1989. Vitray-Meyerovitch, Eva de. *Konya ou la danse cosmique.* Paris: Jacqueline Renard, 1989. Translated into Turkish.

1989. Vitray-Meyerovitch, Eva de, Marc-Alain Descamps, Marie-Madeleine Davy, and Jampa Tartchin. *L'amour transpersonnel.* Lavaur: Trismegiste, 1989.

1990. Jalal-al-din Rumi Maulana. *Lettres.* Translated from the Persian by Eva de Vitray-Meyerovitch. Paris: J. Renard, 1990.

1990. Jalal-al-din Rumi Maulana. *Mathnawi: la quête de l'absolu.* Translated from the original Persian by Eva de Vitray-Meyerovitch and Djamchid Mortazavi. Monaco: Rocher, 1990, 2013.

1991. Vitray-Meyerovitch, Eva de. *L'Islam, l'autre visage*: entretiens avec Rachel et Jean-Pierre Cartier. Paris: Criterion, 1991; Albin Michel, 1995. Translated into Spanish, English, and Turkish.

1991. Shabistari, Mahmud ibn al-Karim. *La Roseraie du mystère.* Translated from the Persian with presentation and notes by Djamchid Mortazavi and Eva de Vitray-Meyerovitch. Paris: Sinbad, 1991; Arles: Actes Sud, 2013.

1992. Zaehner, R.C. *Inde, Israël, Islam: religions mystiques et révélations prophétiques.* Translated from the original English by Eva de Vitray-Meyerovitch. Paris: Desclée De Brouwer, 1992.

1993. Jalal-al-din Rumi Maulana. *Le Chant du Soleil.* Translations by Eva de Vitray-Meyerovitch and Marie-Pierre Chevrier. Paris: Table Ronde, 1993, 1997. Translated into Spanish and Turkish.

1995. Skali, Faouzi et Eva de Vitray-Meyerovitch. *Jésus dans la tradition soufie.* Le Plan-d'Aups: Ed. de l'Ouvert, 1995; Paris: Albin Michel Spiritualités, 2004, 2013. Translated in Italian, Spanish, and Catalan.

1996. Iqbal, Mohammed. *La métaphysique en Perse.* Translated from the original English by Eva de Vitray-Meyerovitch. Paris: Sinbad, 1980; Arles: Actes Sud, 1996.

1996. Iqbal, Mohammed. *Reconstruire la pensée religieuse de l'islam.* Translated from the original English and notes by Eva de Vitray-Meyerovitch. Preface by Louis Massignon. Paris: Adrien-Maisonneuve, 1995; Monaco: Rocher, 1996.

1997. Vitray-Meyerovitch, Eva de. *La Prière en Islam.* With the collaboration of Tewfik Taleb. Paris: Grand Livre du mois, 1997; Albin Michel, 1997, 2003. Translated into Italian and Turkish.

2000. Jalal-al-din Rumi Maulana. *Les quatrains de Rumi.* Translated from the Persian by Eva de Vitray-Meyerovitch. Paris: Albin Michel, 2000.

2001. Gazali, Muhammad ibn Muhammad Abu Hamid al-. *Revivication des sciences de la religion and les secrets de la prière en Islam.* Translated by Eva de Vitray-Meyerovitch and Tewfik Taleb. Beyrouth: al-Bouraq, 2001.

2014. Vitray-Meyerovitch, Eva de. *Universalité de l'Islam.* Commentaires de Jean-Louis Girotto. Paris: Albin Michel, 2014. (Postmortem publication of various articles by Eva de Vitray-Meyerovitch.)